DUE

**Electrical Energy
Management**

Electrical Energy Management

Lawrence J. Vogt
Public Service Indiana

David A. Conner
University of Louisville

Lexington Books
D.C. Heath and Company
Lexington, Massachusetts
Toronto

Library of Congress Cataloging in Publication Data

Vogt, Lawrence J.
    Electrical energy management.

    Bibliography: p.
    Includes index.
    1. Electric power-Conservation. I. Connor, David A., joint author.
II. Title.
TK4015.V63   621.31   77-156
ISBN 0-669-01457-5

Published simultaneously in Canada.

Printed in the United States of America.

International Standard Book Number: 77-156

Library of Congress Catalog Card Number: 0-669-01457-5

To Larry's parents,
Joe and Anne
and to David's wife and parents,
Jerry Ann
Allen and Louise

Contents

List of Figures

List of Tables

Foreword

Electrical Energy Management is a short, readable book that can serve as the working document for developing a company-wide energy management program. It can be a valuable handbook for the beginner in energy management and it can also provide useful guidelines for the experienced practitioner. Topics considered include energy management incentives, electrical load surveys, load management techniques, and programs for energy conservation.

A nation's potential for productivity and a higher living standard are closely tied to effectiveness of energy use. Just as it makes sense economically for the United States to develop and maintain an energy management program, energy management also makes good business sense for a small firm.

Electrical Energy Management is part of a series of books being developed by the Lexington Books Division of D.C. Heath and Company. Subjects stressed are of current interest to electrical engineers, industrial engineers, and engineering managers. This book focuses on implementing an energy management program and on the savings that can be realized by maintaining such a program.

Maurice W. Long

Preface

The Arab oil embargo of 1973 forced our country to take a new look at energy supply and energy usage. In the process, emphasis was placed upon energy conservation in all sectors of society. The natural gas shortage of the winter of 1977 intensified this thrust for energy conservation.

Energy conservation can encompass both the preservation of raw materials and the refinement of energy usage patterns. In the typical industrial setting many raw materials and many energy forms are used. One particular energy form, electrical energy, possesses tremendous potential for conservation measures. This energy form provides the basis for the concepts presented in this book.

Because of their high level of energy consumption, the commercial and industrial sectors have been forced to undertake programs of energy conservation management. Unfortunately, most industries do not possess experts in this field internal to their organizations and have been unable to find resource materials to guide them in initiating such a program.

This book is designed to guide those businesses desiring to initiate energy conservation programs. In particular, the book presents an approach for developing *electrical* energy conservation management programs by discussing how to initiate, design, and implement the programs. Topics considered include energy management incentives, electrical load system survey and analysis approaches, load management techniques, and a review of energy conservation concepts. Emphasis is placed on the energy and monetary savings that evolve from investment in energy management programs.

Electrical Energy Management is written primarily for those at the management level in industry. Managers in the commercial sector might also find this information useful. This book could also be used in the academic setting in courses that emphasize the practical application of management theory.

Acknowledgments

The contribution of the many people who provided valuable inputs during the evolution of this work is deeply appreciated, especially Drs. Joseph D. Cole and Mickey R. Wilhelm of the University of Louisville who contributed their invaluable expertise during all phases of development of this work. Mr. Gary G. Jansen, Mr. Arlis R. Kay, and Mr. Robert W. Thompson of Public Service Indiana provided significant information in the areas of utility load management and industrial power engineering. Mr. Ross Stahl and Mr. Dennis Schaeffer provided the authors with first-hand experience in computerized demand control. The continuous encouragement of Dr. Harry C. Saxe, Dean of the Speed Scientific School of the University of Louisville, should also be noted. Acknowledgment is also in order to Mrs. Rebecca McGaffin, Miss Nancy L. Marks, Miss Connie Wheeler, and Mrs. Donna Greenwell for their secretarial assistance throughout the development of this work, and to Mrs. Jerry Ann Conner for her suggestions relative to grammatical content and her patience with her husband and coauthor as they undertook this work.

Finally, the authors express their thanks to the Kentucky Center for Energy Research and its administrators, Dr. Dee Ashley Akers and Mr. David D. Drake, for their support of this project by funding three project-related trips, and to Frank M. Croft for his contribution in preparing the graphics.

**Electrical Energy
Management**

1   Introduction

The Energy Crisis

After enjoying many years of cheap energy, America has been rudely awakened to the energy crisis. Because of the shortage of primary fuel supplies, the costs of energy have risen at inflationary rates. The economic imbalance and the energy crisis have spawned thousands of new investigations to discover cheaper and/or more efficient fuel sources. In the interim time must be gained by conserving natural resources and managing energy as efficiently as possible.

There are two basic types of fuel in use today—fossil and nuclear fuels. The United States fossil fuel supply will soon dwindle, as shown by table 1-1, even if the energy consumption is kept constant at the current rate.

Dr. Hans A. Bethe, of Cornell University's Laboratory of Nuclear Studies, and thirty-one other scientists report that known U. S. uranium ores possess the energy equivalent to 6000 billion tons of coal while lesser grade ores provide even greater potentials.[1] However, in light of current economic, environmental, and safety interrogations of the nuclear industry, the development of nuclear fuel as a nationwide energy source lags far behind its demand.

Many solutions have been suggested to make the United States energy self-sufficient, but it will be costly years before such independence will come about. The expense of recovering fuels from the earth will continue to increase. Large amounts of capital are needed for the research, development, and demonstration of new energy sources—for example, solar energy. The cost burden will rest heavily on the energy consumer.

Even with consumer cooperation and support, the federal government will play a major role in energy development plans. The government must regulate energy sources so as to balance adequately energy supply and demand. The government must also absorb a significant portion of the financial risk of energy research for several reasons.[2] First, industry will have difficulty raising the entire capital

1

Table 1-1
U.S. Fossil Fuel Supplies

	Known Reserves (recoverable)	Current Annual Production	Years* Supply
Coal	150×10^9 tons	600×10^6 tons	250
Natural gas	1110×10^{12} ft³	23×10^{12} ft³	48
Petroleum oil	190×10^9 bbl	4×10^9 bbl	47
Shale oil	600×10^9 bbl		

Source: Chevron Oil Company, *Energy Conservation Facts*, Section A, p. 3. Reprinted with permission.
*At current rate of consumption.

required for large-scale energy research and development programs that are not currently feasible from a business investment point of view. Second, new technologies introduced into the commercial markets have some degree of uncertainty and risk. Third, energy programs must be developed at an accelerated rate for the ever increasing demand for energy supplies to be satisfied. Management and financing of energy research and development at the federal level will ensure that the programs conducted by industry are those best suited to the nation's interest and well being.

As illustrated by figure 1-1, top management of the Westinghouse Corporation has offered the theory of shifting to an electric economy as a long-term solution to America's energy problem. D.C. Burnham, Westinghouse board chairman, has presented a plan[3] that will be instrumental in bringing about an electric economy. This plan calls for the increased use of atomic energy by means of (a) increasing the number of nuclear power plants, (b) developing the breeder reactor, (c) substituting nuclear-based electricity, where practical, for energy sources in short supply, and (d) developing fusion energy. The plan also includes expanded research, development, and demonstration in the nonnuclear fields of (a) coal gasification and liquefaction; (b) oil shale and tar sands; and (c) geothermal and solar energies.

This scenario suggests operations which are near term (until 1985), midterm (1985 to 2000), and long term (after 2000) in nature. Effective action can be taken immediately through energy conservation measures; thus, conservation is a means of "buying time" while new energy sources are being developed. Since electricity is generated primarily through the combustion of fossil fuels, the

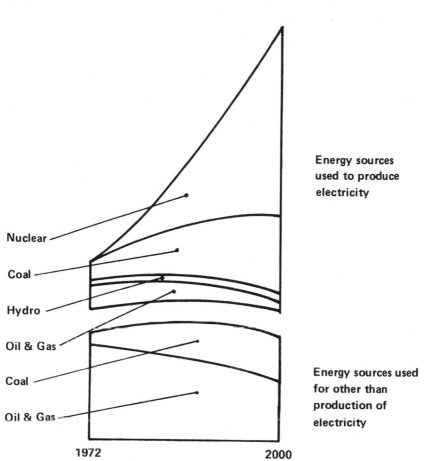

Nuclear

Coal

Hydro

Oil & Gas

Coal

Oil & Gas

Energy sources
used to produce
electricity

Energy sources used
for other than
production of
electricity

1972   2000

Source: Burnham, D.C., "A Shift To An Electric Economy Must Be The Heart of America's Energy Policy," A Westinghouse Advertisement, 1973.

Figure 1-1. Projected Distribution of U.S. Energy Sources in a Shift to an Electric Economy

conservation of electrical energy is a means of preserving these raw fuels. In fact, many electric utilities are marketing the wise and efficient use of electricity as a means of relieving their demand for fuels which are in short supply.

Electrical Energy Conservation

Electrical energy conservation is the reduction of the total kilowatt-hour (energy) consumption by a system or network. Conservation is effected by (a) attenuating or (b) eliminating energy use in various segments or processes within the system. For example, the energy requirement is attenuated or reduced when an old lighting system is revamped with more efficient lamps that require less energy input per light output than the former lamps. The energy requirement is eliminated, at least intermittently, when lamps that were previously burned continuously are used only when actually needed.

Electrical energy conservation affects the consumer economically. Through electric energy conservation the efficiency of energy use is increased, since less energy is used to realize the same end result (for example, product output). The effect is a reduction in charges for electrical energy. In the case of large industries, where the electric bill is computed as a charge for both the energy used (kilowatt-hours) and the peak loading reached during a thirty day billing cycle (kilowatts), several thousands of dollars savings can be realized each month through a carefully implemented conservation plan. This potential savings can serve as an investment incentive to entice top management to participate in energy conservation activities. Once savings are actually realized, these funds could be fed back in support of continuing conservation programs.

The electric utility benefits from customer programs that lower electrical demand. With demand reduced on the electric energy system, especially during extreme peak load periods, there is a capability for normal load growth without the requirement for upgrading of distribution, transmission, and generation equipment. Construction of new facilities could then be allocated over a longer period of time.

Electrical Energy Management

Energy management is defined as the application of the administrative functions of engineering, accounting, purchasing, and finance to energy utilization within a system.[4] Electric energy represents a very large and necessary input to the nation's energy consumers; thus, the management of electricity use holds great potential for both energy and capital savings.

State-of-the-Art

In general, the interest in and practice of all forms of energy management is expanding across the nation. Energy conservation conferences, symposia, and workshops are being conducted around the country to educate and promote expertise in the energy picture.

Most energy management programs for buildings and plants are being designed and applied by in-house personnel. As a result, few publications are available that present a detailed view of energy management theory and application. Those which are available are usually case histories. Current research and development on energy conservation programs is attempting to further the standardization of energy management techniques and procedures.

The energy crisis has prompted consumers to practice conservation by first identifying energy wasters and then taking corrective action. Equipment such as heat recovery devices and electric load controllers are being utilized to increase system efficiency.

New electrical appliances and equipment are being designed and manufactured with emphasis placed on high energy efficiency and low operating expenses. For example, a synchronous clock has been developed that operates on less than five milliamperes of current (which cannot be detected by a conventional watt-hour meter). This new design might seem insignificant, but if all clocks were exchanged for the new design, sufficient electricity would be conserved to light the homes of a city with a population of 250,000 people.[5]

Problem Statement

Electrical energy management is indeed a necessity in combating the energy crisis; however, several tasks must be undertaken to initiate a successful program within a business organization. First, top management must be sold on the idea of energy conservation so that they will give their full support to an energy management program. Second, a large-scale electrical energy management program requires an investigation of all related systems which contribute to the consumption of electrical energy. Personnel having a knowledge of the system structure and characteristics must be trained to survey the system in terms of energy and money wastes. Finally, a systematic approach and analysis method is needed for determining the types of procedures and hardware modifications necessary to optimize system efficiency and minimize operating costs. Energy savings must be equated to dollar savings so as to ensure top management that the program is successful.

Problems often arise while implementing an energy management program. The program must be continually monitored so that savings will be guaranteed. In addition, the energy management program should be designed to recover capital expenses just as would any other business investment. The purpose of this book is to outline how an energy management program can be organized and to present ideas that will lead to an effective industrial program.

Overview

The following chapters provide many of the basic "tools" and concepts required to administer a complete and comprehensive electrical energy management program. The material contained herein is presented in a general fashion so that a program can be tailor made for any individual case through the employment of applicable procedures.

The overall considerations that should be undertaken at the onset of development of an electrical energy management program are presented in chapter 2. Incentives for conservation and organization for effective energy management action are discussed. Although electrical energy is the primary consideration throughout this book, chapter 2 is basic to the structuring of a management program for any form of energy resource.

Chapter 3 investigates a representative selection of electrical loads found in both the private and business communities. Emphasis is placed on the power requirements of the various loads and their efficiencies of energy utilization. Load data and characteristics provide the background necessary to conduct an electrical load survey.

Guidelines for energy auditing or surveying are developed in chapter 4. Formats are suggested for the collection of load performance and system energy consumption data to be used for locating energy waste problem areas. Methods of determining load characteristics are discussed.

Methods of load utilization and control for the purpose of optimizing energy use and reducing demand are presented in chapter 5. Topics discussed include the state-of-the-art load management practices of the electric power industry and impediments to various load management programs.

Chapter 6 offers several energy conservation programs and, where possible, methods of determining their potential monetary and energy savings. These programs have various levels of expense and rates of return. Applicable programs are chosen according to the technical situation requirements and the energy budget constraints.

The actual implementation of the electrical energy management program is discussed in chapter 7. The topics considered include scheduling of conservation programs for implementation, evaluation of savings, and maintenance of the energy management program.

Intended Contribution

The energy crunch has made America aware that energy conservation will be a must for many years to come. *Electrical Energy Management* is intended to serve as both an incentive and a working document for management and engineering personnel by illustrating that energy management is not only a necessity but also a worthy and profitable investment. The procedures and examples contained herein are backed by many of the latest conservation and management theories and practices.

This book is primarily intended to be used as a guideline by commercial, industrial, and governmental establishments that desire an electrical energy conservation plan which is both effective and economical in saving energy. The material presented in this work is meant to be a foundation for further technical development by the reader, since every building and plant is a special case and must be considered individually.

This work will also illustrate to the electric power industry the types of energy conservation efforts being made by their customers. Power company energy consultants can then collaborate with their customers to optimize the efficiency and operation cost of the total electric energy system.

Finally, this work will indicate to the student of engineering and architectural sciences the dire need to consider the real world energy situation in everyday studies and designs. The material will also serve as a reference for further research and development in the area of electrical energy conservation management.

2 Energy Management Considerations

Energy management is an effective means of coping with the high costs and short supplies of energy. Voluntary conservation is widely accepted by the private and business communities because of the large potential for savings. A successful energy management program depends on the commitment and organization of all involved parties.

The topics presented in this chapter include incentives for electrical energy conservation and top-level management commitment to energy conservation programs. Committee organization for large-scale business energy programs also is discussed.

Conservation Incentives

The responsibility of energy conservation must be shared by all; however, as shown in table 2-1, the greatest energy savings can be realized by the business community, which accounts for 70 percent of all forms of energy consumed in the United States. Many commercial and industrial establishments throughout the nation have already initiated various types of energy management programs. Many case histories have shown that energy savings on the order of 20 to 30 percent are being realized through carefully managed energy conservation schemes.[1] Because of the inflationary costs of energy, the decision to activate conservation measures has often been based on the monetary savings that can be realized by the investment in energy programs.

Energy Conservation and Savings

Energy management programs may be developed at minimal cost or at high levels of investment. The degree of involvement by a business in a conservation plan is primarily constrained by the budget; however, programs can be designed and implemented with immediate energy savings and desirable rates of return.

9

Table 2-1
U.S. Energy Consumption—By Application

Private Sector (%)		Business Sector (%)	
Residential	19	Industrial	43
Transportation	11	Commercial	14
		Transportation	13

Source: U.S. Department of Commerce, "Industry's Vital Stake in Energy Management," Washington, D.C., Government Printing Office, May 1974.

Sometimes "hidden" savings are realized through the execution of an electrical energy conservation plan. For example, large buildings often have air conditioning systems which utilize natural-gas-fired reheat devices at the point of final air delivery. Reduction of the heating load on the air conditioning cooling coils (without appreciably affecting comfort) lessens the cooling requirement; thus, electrical energy is conserved. As an additional result, the reheat units operate less often, thereby conserving natural gas.

Power Utility Rate Schedules

A study of the electric service contract will often aid in determining the types of electrical energy programs that would be economically feasible to implement. For example, many industrial power contracts include penalties for poor power factor. (Power factor is discussed in chapter 3.) Power factor correction not only aids the electrical system but also reduces the monthly power bill by a considerable amount. A copy of the rate structure should be obtained from the local utility so that potential savings studies can be made.

The energy charge for kilowatt-hour consumption and for the fuel adjustment clause is basic to most power bills. Usually the total monthly kilowatt-hours are grouped into "blocks" of kilowatt-hours determined by the rate schedule. The price per kilowatt-hour generally decreases with succeeding blocks (that is, with increasing quantities of kilowatt-hours). The fuel adjustment charge, which is based on the total number of kilowatt-hours consumed, aids the utility in recovering inflationary operating fuel costs.

Electric bills for large commercial and industrial customers also include a demand charge, which is intended to recover the fixed cost of the utility's investment that is needed to supply adequately the power required during peak load periods. As with energy charges, demand charges are sometimes billed for blocks of power in kilowatts or kilovolt-amperes based on the maximum level of power reached during the monthly billing cycle. Sometimes demand is billed on a monthly minimum charge or "rachet rate" in that charges based on an established maximum demand remain in effect for the following eleven months unless a still higher maximum is achieved.

Electric service rate structures vary among power companies. For example, electric service tariffs for customers in areas where hydroelectric generation is predominant (such as in parts of Canada and the American northwest) typically do not include energy charges. This procedure is based on the philosophy that energy obtained from falling water is "free"; therefore, capital costs are recovered through demand charges.[2]

Cautions on Energy Management Systems

Constraints should be established before making large capital investments in energy management programs, equipment, and systems. Consideration should be given to the authenticity of energy management system operators, suppliers, and promoters. Energy projects will not be effective if implemented by irresponsible or unknowledgeable personnel. Successful savings are best ensured by investment in programs and systems that have been engineered by the respected leaders in the energy management business. The energy services department of the local electric utility or of private consultants should be consulted to determine which energy programs will promote the most efficient use of electricity. These considerations[3] stress the need for cooperation among all who are involved, whether directly or indirectly, in the area of energy conservation management.

Top-Level Management Commitment

For a large-scale energy management program to succeed, it must have the endorsement and the support of top management. Management must allocate resources and delegate authority to the line personnel who develop and execute the program. Management should set measurable goals for energy conservation and money savings and develop guidelines, standards, and policies so that conservation efforts will be uniform.

Many large companies have created energy committees at the corporate level to act in an advisory capacity. This committee is chaired by a corporate official and composed of both management and technically oriented personnel. Such a committee's responsibilities could include the following tasks:[4]

1. Assess the availability of energy supplies and alternatives (including standby services);
2. Originate programs best suited to the corporation's energy needs;
3. Coordinate and advise corporate energy subcommittees (that is, plant-level energy committees);
4. Monitor governmental directives and regulations which affect energy resources;
5. Document corporate energy activities; and
6. Collaborate with personnel from other businesses to develop and distribute energy management technologies.

Plant-Level Energy Committee

A committee should be established at the plant level by the corporate committee to initiate actual energy conservation action. The plant-level committee should be chaired by a plant officer who can correspond directly with top management. Committee members should be composed of the in-house or local expertise from each department (that is, engineering, maintenance, etc.). The duties[5] of this committee could include the actual design and implementation of the energy programs offered by the corporate level committee. The plant committee would also provide the corporate committee input concerning local energy supply availability and any special problems encountered.

Energy Management Program Resources

All plants might not have on hand the total expertise required to initiate an energy management program. At plants where utilization energy management technology is still quite "new," assistance may be obtained from out-of-house experts who are proficient in energy management. Such expertise may come from:

1. Consulting engineers,
2. Public service utilities and commissions,
3. Manufacturers of energy management systems,
4. Institutes of engineering technology,
5. Professional societies, associations, and institutions,
6. The United States Department of Commerce,
7. The Energy Research and Development Administration,
8. The Federal Energy Administration, or
9. Other related federal, state, and local agencies.

Organizational Summary

The process of organizing personnel and distributing responsibilities to establish a large-scale energy management program within a business is suggested by a Delta chart (figure 2-1). The Delta chart, which is typically used in planning functions, is a modification of the flow chart used in computer programming. The Delta chart was originated because of the need for an improved technique of illustrating a logical scheme of activities in various research and development projects.[6] Delta charts might also be used to define details within individual energy conservation programs.

Summary

The greatest potential for energy savings lies in the industrial and commercial sectors. The incentive to conserve is primarily one of economics as rising energy costs justify investment in conservation programs. Energy management programs are effective in reducing energy consumption, often by drastic quantities.

For a business to implement such programs, top management endorsement and support must be acquired. In large companies, energy committees may be established to initiate and monitor conservation actions. As with any other business endeavor, organization of personnel and job functions is essential for a successful energy management program.

14

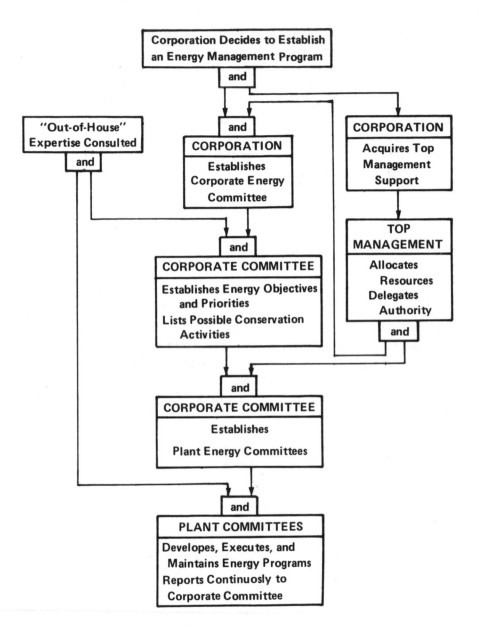

Figure 2-1. Delta Chart of Energy Management Organization

Once commitment and organization for electrical energy management are established, an energy survey of the electrical system must be taken to determine energy consumption behavior and the potential for savings. Chapter 3 investigates many of the electrical energy consuming devices situated in the business community with emphasis placed on energy consumption and utilization characteristics. Chapter 4 then incorporates this information in a discussion on energy surveying or auditing.

3 Electrical Load Analysis

An electrical energy management program requires an understanding of the energy utilization devices that constitute a system. The particular traits of the individual components or loads characterize the system energy consumption behavior. The topics discussed in this chapter provide much of the background needed to document energy flows and utilization within an electrical system.

The term *load* refers to a device that is connected to and draws power from the electric energy supply network for the purpose of power transformation or conversion. Loads are usually rated in size by the level of power at which they operate, typically volt-amperes or watts. Loads may have a single-phase or multiphase symmetry, a real or complex impedance, and either a continuous or an intermittent time period of operation, depending on their applications.

Types of Loads—Energy Considerations

Loads are energy conversion devices that transform electrical energy into other forms such as chemical energy (as in battery charging), thermal energy (as in resistance heating), or mechanical energy (as in motors). Power losses are present in the transformation; therefore, each load has an efficiency rating given by

$$\text{Efficiency} = \frac{\text{Power Output}}{\text{Power Input}} \qquad (3.1a)$$

$$= \frac{\text{Power Input} - \text{Power Losses}}{\text{Power Input}}. \qquad (3.1b)$$

Generation efficiency is the efficiency achieved in the actual energy conversion process. System efficiency, on the other hand, is the efficiency achieved by a system which contains an energy conversion process. For example, a hot water heater contains a set of resistance

17

elements that convert electrical energy to heat energy at a rather high conversion or generation efficiency. Heat losses in the water pipes and heater components provide a system efficiency less than that of the generation efficiency. The total losses in a building or plant can amount to a considerable waste in electrical energy and thus money.

Loads are typically divided into two categories—lighting loads and power loads. The following treatment of these categories will be in terms of their energy requirements and efficiencies of operation. Note that the efficiency of some of these loads, by definition, is a ratio having dimensions (for example, Btu/Hr:Watt) as opposed to a ratio in percent.

Lighting Loads

Over 20 percent of the electrical energy generated for all uses in the United States in 1972 was consumed by direct lighting. This consumption represents 360 billion kilowatt-hours or 5 percent of the total energy consumed in the United States. Nearly 70 percent of total lighting energy usage may be attributed to commercial, public, and industrial buildings.[1]

The efficiencies of the principle types of electric lamps in use are shown in table 3-1. Lighting efficiency is measured by lumens per watt, where a lumen is the measure of light flux (one lumen is equal to 0.00413 watt). Table 3-1 shows that the sodium vapor lamp is the most efficient lamp available today. The use of sodium vapor lighting is becoming an increasingly popular energy conservation measure.

Table 3-1
Primary Types of Electrical Lamps

Type of Light Source	Typical Efficiencies (Lumens/Watt)
Carbon filament	4
Tantalum filament	6
Tungsten filament	35
Mercury vapor	60
Fluorescent	80
Metal halide	90
Sodium vapor	105

Source: General Electric Company, "High Intensity Discharge Lamps," TP-109, Cleveland, August 1971, p. 4.

Incandescent Lighting. Incandescent illumination is based on the radiation of light energy when an electric current is conducted through a filament, usually made of tungsten. Incandescent lighting is the least efficient of the principle types of electric lighting. The efficiencies of several incandescent lamps are shown in table 3-2. As indicated by table 3-2, the efficiency of an incandescent lamp generally increases with increasing bulb wattage.

The input energy to the filament is dissipated as useful light and as heat losses. A 40-watt incandescent bulb would have an energy distribution as approximated in figure 3-1. Heat loss is accounted for (a) by radiation of infrared heat along with the light and (b) by heat absorption by the bulb's components and internal gas.

Fluorescent Lighting. Fluorescence is based on a low voltage electric discharge through a low pressure mercury vapor atmosphere. This phenomenon transforms approximately 60 percent of the input wattage to radiation having a wavelength of 2537 angstroms, where one angstrom is equal to 10^{-8} centimeters.[2] A phosphor coating on the inside of the tube converts the radiation to visible light.

The efficiencies of several fluorescent lamps are shown in table

Table 3-2
Various Characteristics of Selected Incandescent Lamps

Lamp Watts	Approximate Initial Lumens	Rated Initial Lumens/Watt
10	80	8.0
15	126	8.4
25	230	9.2
40	455	11.4
50	680	13.6
60	860	14.3
75	1180	15.7
100	1740	17.2
150	2880	19.2
200	4000	20.0

Source: J.E. Kaufman, ed., *IES Lighting Handbook*, Illuminating Engineering Society, 5th ed., 1972, Section 8, p. 57. Reprinted with permission.

Note: Characteristics of the type noted here are continually changing as new innovations develop with respect to lamp design. A lamp supplier should be consulted for the most current data.

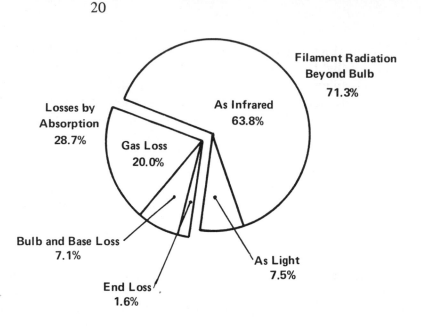

Source: Based on Harold Pender and William A. Del Mar, *Electrical Engineer's Handbook Electric Power*, 4th ed., New York, John Wiley and Son's Inc., 1949, Section 15, p. 12.

Figure 3-1. Luminous and Thermal Characteristics of a 40-Watt Incandescent Bulb

3-3. In comparison to incandescent lighting, fluorescent lighting is about four to five times more efficient. For example, a 15-watt incandescent bulb from table 3-2 has an efficiency of only 8.4 lumens per watt; whereas a fluorescent lamp of the same wattage has an efficiency of 44.1 lumens per watt.

The total operating wattage of the fluorescent fixture is increased above the nominal lamp wattage by the power requirements of the ballast. The distribution of input energy in a 40-watt fluorescent lamp is illustrated in figure 3-2. As with incandescent lamps, most of the input energy is dissipated as heat, which is radiated with the light and absorbed by the lamp fixture components.

High Intensity Discharge Lighting. Unlike fluorescent lamps, high intensity discharge lamps are constructed of small-volume arc tubes containing "high pressure" vapors that are only a few times greater than normal atmospheric pressure. The three common types of high intensity discharge lamps are based upon the type of arc material

Table 3-3
Various Characteristics of Selected Fluorescent Lamps

Lamp Watts	Ballast Watts	Total Watts	Initial Lumens[a]	Rated Initial Lumens/Watt[b]
4.5	2	6.5	125	19.2
6	2	8	265	33.1
7.2	2	9.2	400	43.5
14.3	5.5	19.8	675	34.1
15	4.5	19.5	860	44.1
20	5	25	1250	50.0
26	6	32	1815	56.7
30	10.5	40.5	2190	54.1
40	12	52	3200	61.5
90	20	110	6350	57.7

Source: J.E. Kaufman, ed., *IES Lighting Handbook*, Illuminating Engineering Society, 5th ed., 1972, Section 8, pp. 96, 101. Reprinted with permission.

Note: Characteristics of the type noted here are continually changing as new innovations develop with respect to lamp design. A lamp supplier should be consulted for the most current data.

[a]Cool white.
[b]Total watts.

used. These arc materials are (a) mercury, (b) mercury and metallic iodides, and (c) sodium/mercury amalgam.

The General Electric Company is a representative example of a manufacturer of high intensity discharge lamps. General Electric has manufactured mercury vapor lamps with efficiencies ranging from 35 to 60 lumens per watt, metal halide (Multi-Vapor) lamps with efficiencies ranging from 80 to 90 lumens per watt, and sodium vapor (Lucalox) lamps with an efficiency of 105 lumens per watt.[3]

As with incandescent and fluorescent lamps, high intensity discharge lamps have power losses that are attributed to heat. The input power distributions of General Electric's mercury vapor, metal halide, and sodium vapor lamps—each rated at 400 watts—are shown in table 3-4.

Power Loads

Power loads are all loads other than lighting. These loads may be classified as either residential and small commercial loads *or* indus-

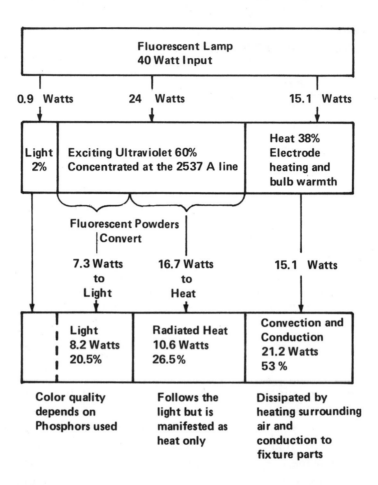

Source: Harold Pender and William A. Del Mar, *Electrical Engineer's Handbook Electric Power*, 4th ed., New York, John Wiley and Son's, Inc., 1949, Section 15, p. 30. Reprinted with permission.

Figure 3-2. Energy Input and Conversion in the 40-Watt Standard Fluorescent Lamp

trial and large commercial loads. Residential loads typically consist of appliances and comfort conditioning (that is, heating and cooling) devices; whereas industrial and commercial loads are normally large energy-consuming devices that are utilized in a large-scale production setting. Loads situated in governmental installations are primarily the same as those found in commercial and industrial facilities.

Table 3-4
Distribution of Power Input to Typical 400-Watt High Intensity Discharge Lamps

	Radiated Watts			Watts Conducted and Convected
Lamp Type	Ultraviolet (less than 380 nm)	Light (380-760 nm)	Infrared (greater than 760 nm)	
Mercury	8.3	64.3	207.4	120
Multivapor[a]	12.5	95.4	148.1	144
Lucalox[a]	0.8	120.0	175.2	104

Source: General Electric Company, "High Intensity Discharge Lamps," TP-109, Cleveland, August 1971, p. 25. Reprinted with permission.
[a]Trade-name of the General Electric Company.

Appliances. A comprehensive listing of common appliances, including their average power ratings and estimated annual energy consumption, is shown in table 3-5. The annual energy consumption estimate is based on normal usage. For example, a radio-record player is assigned an average wattage of 109 watts or 0.109 kilowatts; thus, the estimate of 109 kilowatt-hours consumption per year is based on an assumed usage of 1000 hours annually. However, for accurate projections, the actual (nameplate) wattage of each appliance and the particular usage characteristics should be considered.

In an effort to encourage the manufacture and use of more energy-efficient appliances, the Department of Commerce, in conjunction with the Council on Environmental Quality and the Environmental Protection Agency, has developed a voluntary three-part energy conservation labeling program[4] for the manufacturing, retail sales, and consumer groups. Manufacturers will provide product information that denotes the energy requirements and efficiencies of operation in comparison to competitive designs. Retail merchants will market the program within their outlets by providing the public with literature about energy labeling. Consumers can then encourage manufacturers to compete in the energy design of products by purchasing the most efficient appliances.

Electric Resistance Space Heating. The process of resistance heating is based on the passage of current through a resistance element with the power being dissipated as heat. The power is given by

Table 3-5
Approximate Wattage Rating and Estimated Annual KWH Consumption of Electrical Appliances

Appliance	Average Wattage	Estimated Annual KWH Consumption
Food preparation		
Blender	300	1
Broiler	1,140	85
Carving knife	92	8
Coffee maker	894	106
Deep fryer	1,448	83
Dishwasher	1,201	363
Egg cooker	516	14
Frying pan	1,196	100
Hot plate	1,200	90
Mixer	127	2
Oven, microwave (only)	1,450	190
Range		
with oven	12,200	1,175
with self-cleaning oven	12,200	1,205
Roaster	1,333	60
Sandwich grill	1,161	33
Toaster	1,146	39
Trash compactor	400	50
Waffle iron	1,200	20
Waste dispenser	445	7
Food preservation		
Freezer (15-21 ft^3)		
Chest-type, manual defrost		1,320
Upright-type		
Manual defrost		1,320
Automatic defrost		1,985
Refrigerators/Freezers		
Manual defrost (10-15 ft^3)		700
Automatic defrost (16-18 ft^3)		1,795
Automatic defrost (20 ft^3 & up)		1,895
Laundry		
Clothes dryer	4,856	993
Iron (hand)	1,100	60
Washing machine (automatic)	512	103
Washing machine (nonautomatic)	286	76
Water heater	2,475	4,219
(quick recovery)	4,474	4,811

Table 3-5 (cont.)

Appliance	Average Wattage	Estimated Annual KWH Consumption
Comfort conditioning		
Air cleaner	50	216
Air conditioner (room)	860	860
Bed covering	177	147
Dehumidifier	257	377
Fan (attic)	370	291
Fan (circulating)	88	43
Fan (rollaway)	171	138
Fan (window)	200	170
Heater (portable)	1,322	176
Heating pad	65	10
Humidifier	177	163
Health & Beauty		
Germicidal lamp	20	141
Hair dryer	381	14
Heat lamp (infrared)	250	13
Shaver	15	0.5
Sun lamp	279	16
Tooth brush	1.1	1.0
Vibrator	40	2
Home entertainment		
Radio	71	86
Radio/Record player	109	109
Television		
Black & white		
Tube-type	100	220
Solid-state	45	100
Color		
Tube-type	240	528
Solid-state	145	320
Housewares		
Clock	2	17
Floor polisher	305	15
Sewing machine	75	11
Vacuum cleaner	630	46

Source: Edison Electric Institute, "Annual Energy Requirements of Electric Household Appliances," New York, 1975. Reprinted with permission.

$$P = I^2R = E^2/R \qquad (3.2)$$

where P is the power in watts, I is the load current in amperes (the rms value if the current is time-variant), R is the resistance in ohms of the load (that is, heater element), and E is the voltage applied across the load.

Typical resistor materials are nickel-chromium and various ferro-alloys. These materials are employed in various forms of heating installations, including

1. Wall, ceiling, and baseboard units,
2. Duct insert and infrared radiant heaters, and
3. Heating cables.

Space heating furnaces similarly use resistance materials in conjunction with blowers, filters, and controls.

The conversion of electric energy to heat energy via electric resistance heating is for all practical purposes 100 percent efficient. The annual energy or kilowatt-hour consumption required by the heating device depends upon the desired indoor temperature, the heat loss of the structure, and the geographical climate conditions.

Air Conditioning. Air conditioning is the process of cooling, dehumidifying, and purifying the atmosphere within a conditioned space to provide climate for humans, animals, plants, or perishable goods.[5] The cooling capacity of an air conditioner is rated in Btu per hour, where 12,000 Btu per hour is equal to one ton of refrigeration. For example, a 4000 Btu air conditioner would remove approximately 4000 Btu of heat each hour from the conditioned space.

Air conditioning units are assigned an energy efficiency ratio (EER). This ratio is obtained by dividing the Btu per hour rating by the power input rating as given by

$$\text{EER} = \frac{\text{Btu/Hr Output}}{\text{Watts Input}}. \qquad (3.3)$$

(Thus EER has the dimensions of Btu per watt-hour.) The higher the EER, the more efficient the unit.

The performance data for several air conditioning units having various rated cooling capacities is shown in table 3-6. The EER

Table 3-6
Variations in Performance of Selected Air Conditioners

Rated Cooling Capacity (Btu)	Nominal Rated Current Demand (amperes)	Energy Efficiency Ratio (Btu/hr per watt)
4,000	8.8	3.96
	7.5	4.65
	5.0	6.96
5,000	9.5	4.58
	7.5	5.80
	5.0	8.70
6,000	9.1	5.34
	7.5	6.96
8,000	12.0	5.80
24,000	17.0	5.85
	15.4	7.10
	13.1	8.25

Source: *Energy Alternatives: A Comparative Analysis,* Catalog Number PREX 14.2:EN2, Washington, D.C., Government Printing Office, May 1975, Section 13, p. 12.

generally increases with decreasing load current. As with electrical resistance heating, the annual kilowatt-hour consumption required by the cooling unit depends upon the desired indoor temperature, the heat gain of the structure, and the geographical climate conditions.

Electric Heat Pump. The heat pump integrates the function of both heating and cooling into one system. By the fundamental laws of thermodynamics, heat flows from an area of higher concentration (heat source) to an area of lower concentration (heat sink); however, the heat pump consumes electrical energy to transfer heat from lower to higher concentrations. In summer, the pump removes heat and humidity from indoors and expels it to an outside medium which is air, earth, or water. In winter, the pump extracts heat from the outside medium and transfers it indoors.

The instantaneous efficiency of a heat pump system is signified by the coefficient of performance (COP), the ratio of the thermal energy output to the heat equivalent of the electrical energy (KWH) input given by

$$COP = \frac{Btu/Hr\ Output}{KW\ Input \times 3413\ Btu/KWH} \cdot \qquad (3.4)$$

Heat pump performance data for various sources and sinks is shown in table 3-7. The greatest efficiency is achieved when water (such as well water) is used for the outside medium.

However, to determine the annual efficiency of the heat pump, the Seasonal Performance Factor (SPF) is calculated. The SPF is the ratio of the net annual heating requirements (including operation of the pump's supplemental resistance heaters) to the net electrical energy input during the heating season. The SPF will vary because of such factors as the size and model of pump, the geographical climate conditions, and the type of auxiliary resistance heater design.[6]

Comfort Conditioning Systems. In large buildings, the comfort conditioning processes are typically centralized into heating, ventilating, and air conditioning (HVAC) systems. In figure 3-3, the HVAC system is divided into three principle zones of operation and control. Proper setting of controls in each of these areas is essential for optimum operating efficiency of the HVAC system. Annual energy requirements of HVAC comfort conditioning systems are analogous to the heating and cooling devices that have been discussed earlier.

Refrigeration and Chillers. The term refrigeration is primarily applied to the cooling of perishable foods and beverages and to the production of ice. Table 3-8 shows the energy required to produce 100 pounds of ice at various delivery water temperatures. Naturally,

Table 3-7
Coefficients of Performance for Electrically Driven Heat Pumps with Various Sources and Sinks

	Coefficient of Performance	
Source and Sink	Heating	Cooling
Air	2.5	3.0
Water	5.0	4.0
Earth	3.0	3.0

Source: *Energy Alternatives: A Comparative Analysis*, Catalog Number PREX 14.2:EN2, Washington, D.C., Government Printing Office, May 1975, Section 13, p. 8.

Pre-Conditioning	Controlled Conditioning	Final Delivery
Ventilating Filtering Pre-Heating Heat Reclamation Odor Control	Heating Cooling Humidifying De-Humidifying	Re-Heat Re-Cool Volume

Source: Honeywell, Inc., *Energy Conservation Management Workshop*, Minneapolis, 1975, Section V-A, p. 17. Reprinted with permission.

Figure 3-3. Control Applications for HVAC Systems

the energy required to form ice increases with the temperature of the delivery water. An efficiency of approximately 50 percent is typical for electric refrigeration equipment.[7]

Chillers are used for cooling large quantities of water or brine. The energy consumption for electric drive chillers will vary with cooling capacity. The input power is typically 0.77 KW to 0.93 KW per ton. However, the power requirements for the complete chiller unit (including electric-driven pumps) can be estimated by 1 kilowatt per ton.[8]

Electric Hot Water Heating and Boilers. Electric heating is commonly used for the purpose of generating hot water and steam. There are two basic types of boilers—the immersion element and the electrode. Immersion element boilers transfer thermal energy, by conduction, from a set of electrical resistance heater elements, through a protective sleeve, to the water. On the other hand, electrode boilers generate heat, via the I^2R effect, by conducting electricity between electrodes through the water itself. No heat is lost in the transfer process; thus, like space heating, the conversion or generation efficiency of the electrode boiler is 100 percent.[9] Based on this conversion efficiency of 100 percent, the temperature of 4.1 gallons of water will be increased by 100° Fahrenheit for each kilowatt-hour applied.[10] The amount of energy consumption by the heating unit

Table 3-8
Energy Consumed in Making Ice

Temperature of water	60°F	65°F	70°F	75°F	80°F
Kilowatt hours per 100 lb. of ice	5.35	5.54	5.75	5.99	6.25

Source: Edison Electric Institute, *Electric Application Handbook for Commercial Salesmen*, New York, 1972, Section VIII, p. 7. Reprinted with permission.

depends upon the quantity of water heated, the initial and final water temperatures, and the thermal losses of the heating unit system.

Electric Heating, Furnaces, and Ovens. Electricity is utilized in many large-scale heating processes, including

1. Resistance heating,
2. Arc heating,
3. Induction heating,
4. Dielectric heating.

As with other types of devices which convert electrical energy to heat energy, the generation efficiency of industrial furnaces and ovens is approximately 100 percent.

In resistance and arc furnaces, heating may result by the direct application of current to the charge or work piece. With resistance heating, current is applied directly to the work piece via electrodes. The work piece provides a resistive path to the current flow, with heating taking place by the I^2R effect. On the other hand, arc heating utilizes electrodes that are normally situated above the charge. Heat is generated by an arc sustained between the tip of each electrode (one per phase) and the charge.

Heating may also result from currents being induced in the charge as in the induction furnace. The furnace basically consists of an induction coil and a chamber which contains the molten metal. Induction furnaces are of either the channel type or the coreless type. With the channel furnace, the melt flows within a channel that encircles the primary circuit. With the coreless furnace, the melt is contained within a vessel that is surrounded by a cylindrical primary coil. The intense electromagnetic forces induce a dense current flow in the melt, thereby producing heat.

Sixty Hertz operation is most common for industrial furnaces; however, some furnaces operate at higher or lower frequencies. In the latter cases, frequencies are obtained by conversion of a 60 Hertz input via motor-generator sets or electronic oscillators. Overall operating efficiencies can be achieved in excess of 75 percent with motor-generator sets and near 50 percent with electronic oscillators.[11]

A special case of heating occurs with dielectric or capacitance heating. Electrostatic fields are used to generate heat in a material placed between two symmetrical plates. A high frequency field applied between the plates causes distortions in the molecular structure of the material; thus, heat is produced internally. An overall operating efficiency of approximately 50 percent can be achieved with dielectric heating.[12]

Ovens are normally considered to be heating devices which operate at temperatures lower than furnaces with the dividing line being 1000° Fahrenheit.[13] Two types of resistor ovens are commonly used—convection and radiation ovens. Convection ovens are based on the transfer of heat by forced convection in a gaseous environment, accomplished by a fan and a set of resistance heating elements. Radiation ovens function by heat transfer from tungsten-filament lamps which generate large amounts of infrared radiation.

Electric Motors. Many appliances and electric machines already discussed employ motor drives. For accuracy, the power requirements of associated motors must be considered when reviewing electrical equipment. The power consumption of electric motors can be estimated by 0.766 kilowatts per horsepower. Such an approximation is based on a power factor of 90 percent and an efficiency of 92 percent with loading being 85 percent of the nameplate rating of the motor.[14] Motors generally operate efficiently except at light load.

All motors are composed of (a) a stator or stationary part and (b) a rotor in which torque is developed to drive a mechanical load. The basic type of alternating current motors are induction and synchronous motors.

In the induction motor, current is applied directly to the stator windings, thus causing a rotating magnemotive force (mmf) wave. Rotor current generated by induction from the stator also causes a rotating magnemotive force wave. These waves rotate in synchronism within the rotor-stator air gap despite the actual rotor speed. The induction process is analogous to transformer action. Induction motor rotors are of either the wound type or the squirrel-cage type.

In the synchronous motor, alternating current is supplied to the stator windings, thus causing a rotating mmf wave. Direct current, generated by an exciter, is supplied to the rotor windings via slip rings, thus causing an mmf wave whose rotation is dependent on the speed of the rotor. Therefore, the actual rotor speed must turn with the rotation of the stator wave for the mmf waves to travel in synchronism.

As illustrated by figure 3-4, the general application of synchronous motors is based on the horsepower and motor rpm requirements. Because of difficulties in motor manufacturing for certain motor size ratings at various voltage levels, voltage also serves as a criterion for motor applications.[15] Table 3-9 indicates the minimum horsepower ratings that should be applied for various motors. Within a given voltage range, horsepower generally decreases with speed.

Motor service life is determined in many cases by the number of starts rather than the total hours of operation. A quick succession of start/stops may reduce motor life or cause damaging stresses. When a motor is energized, the internal conductors are subjected to an inrush (locked rotor) current. This starting current, which is momentary in nature to produce sufficient starting torque, is usually several times greater than the full load running current. Full load currents for various three-phase synchronous and induction motors are shown in tables 3-10 and 3-11.

Load Requirements

Electrical loads are dependent on service quality. Variations in frequency and voltage affect the real and reactive power flow to the load. Devices such as data processing systems are sensitive to voltage surges and transients. Many alternating current machines operate with mechanical speeds that are directly proportional to line frequency.

Loads also require a degree of service dependability. Generally, a service discontinuity causes discomfort or inconvenience. In the industrial sector where many processes are dependent on electricity, loss of power, even for a short time, can possibly result in equipment and/or production material damage. An unplanned shutdown of production equipment results in a monetary loss.

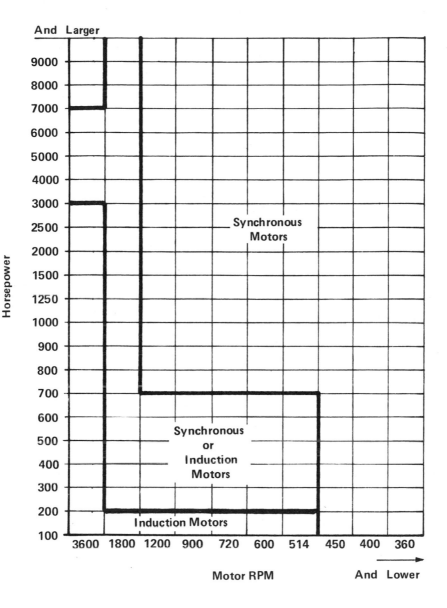

Source: G.L. Oscarson, *ABC of Large AC Motors and Control*, Electric Machinery Manufacturing Co., 1973, Part 1, Fundamentals, p. 33. Reprinted with permission.

Figure 3-4. General Areas of Application of Synchronous Motors and Induction Motors

Table 3-9
Minimum Recommended Motor Rating—HP versus Volts

Volts	rpm	Induction	Synchronous
601– 3,000	3,600	250	
	1,800 or less	250	250
3,001– 5,000	3,600	350	
	1,800 or less	300	250
5,001– 7,000	3,600	1,000	
	1,800 or less	800	600
7,001–13,800	3,600		2,500
	1,800 to 1,200	5,000	2,000
	900 or less	3,000	2,000

Source: G. L. Oscarson, *ABC of Large Motors and Control*, Electric Machinery Manufacturing Co., 1973, Part 2, Applications, p. 5. Reprinted with permission.

The electric energy supply system must be capable of providing reliable service. Properly sized distribution and transmission lines and equipment are necessary to minimize system energy losses. This equipment must have the ability to provide the reliable power required by the load centers during peak periods.

Load Characteristics

The individual loads previously discussed operate together in groups to form systems of composite loads. In light of the electric energy supply system, composite loads are best "viewed" from a strategic location such as the user's metering point, a substation bus, or even the generator. Although a composite load system is unique, its behavior is not totally unpredictable. The following subsections characterize various "views" of a system load.

Connected Load and Diversity

The connected load is the sum of the full load (nameplate) continuous ratings of all electrical devices in the composite load system. Ratings are typically given in watts or kilowatts; however, volt-amperes, horsepower, or full load current ratings are also often used.

It is unlikely that the total connected load of a system would be operational at one time (for example, air conditioning and heating

Table 3-10
Approximate Full Load Amperes of Three-Phase Synchronous Motors

Motor hp	Assumed Efficiency	208 Volts 100% PF	208 Volts 80% PF	220 Volts 100% PF	220 Volts 80% PF	440 Volts 100% PF	440 Volts 80% PF	550 Volts 100% PF	550 Volts 80% PF	2300 Volts 100% PF	2300 Volts 80% PF	4160 Volts 100% PF	4160 Volts 80% PF
50	89.5	116	144	110	136	55	69	44	55	10.5	13.1	5.8	7.3
60	90.0	138	172	130	162	65	82	52	65	12.4	16	6.9	8.6
75	91.0	170	213	162	201	81	101	65	81	15.5	19.4	8.6	10.7
100	91.5	226	283	214	268	107	133	86	107	20.5	25.6	11.4	14
125	91.5	283	354	268	334	133	167	107	133	26	32.0	14	17.7
150	92.0	338	422	320	398	160	200	127	160	31	38	17	21
175	92.0	394	492	373	465	186	233	149	186	36	45	20	25
200	92.0	449	563	426	532	213	266	170	213	41	51	22.5	28
225	92.5	502	630	475	594	238	297	190	238	46	57.0	25	31.5
250	92.5	560	700	529	661	265	331	212	265	51	63.5	28	35
300	92.5	672	840	634	794	317	397	255	317	61	76	34	42
350	93.5	775	970	733	916	366	458	293	366	70	88	39	49
400	93.5	885	1110	838	1046	418	523	335	418	80	100	44	55
450	93.5	995	1246	942	1180	471	590	378	471	90	112	50	62
500	94.0	1102	1376	1042	1302	520	652	418	520	100	125	55	69
600	94.0	1323	1654	1250	1563	625	780	500	625	120	149	66	83
700	94.5	1535	1917	1450	1813	725	907	580	725	139	174	76	96
800	95.0	1745	2185	1650	2060	824	1030	659	824	158	198	87	109
900	95.0	1960	2452	1855	2320	928	1160	741	928	177	221	98	122
1000	95.0	2180	2723	2060	2580	1030	1290	825	1030	197	246	109	136
1250	95.0	2720	3405	2572	3220	1290	1610	1030	1290	247	308	136	170
1500	95.0					1545	1933	1236	1545	296	370	163	204
1750	95.0					1800	2255	1444	1800	345	431	191	239
2000	95.5					2050	2665	1640	2050	392	490	217	271
2250	95.5									441	551	244	305
2500	95.5									490	613	271	340
3000	96.0									585	731	324	404
3500	96.0									682	853	377	472

Source: G. L. Oscarson, *ABC of Large AC Motors and Control*, Machinery Manufacturing Co., 1973, Part 3, Controls, p. 15. Reprinted with permission.

Table 3-11
Approximate Full Load Amperes of Three-Phase Induction Motors

Motor hp	Assumed Efficiency	Assumed Power Factor	Voltage				
			208	220	440	2300	4160
30	87.0	79.0	90.5	85.5	42.8		
40	87.5	80.0	118	112	56.0		
50	87.7	80.5	147	139	69.5	13.3	
60	87.9	81.0	175	165	82.6	15.8	
75	88.5	83.5	211	199	99.5	19.0	
100	89.2	84.7	274	260	130	24.8	13.9
125	90.2	86.5	333	314	157	30.0	16.7
150	90.7	87.2	393	372	186	35.5	19.7
200	91.6	88.5	511	483	242	46.3	25.7
250	92.0	86.0			310	59.1	32.9
300	92.4	86.0			370	70.8	39.3
350	92.7	86.5			428	81.9	45.5
400	92.9	87.0			485	92.7	51.4
450	93.1	87.2			542	104	57.6
500	93.2	88.0			597	114	63.4
600	93.5	88.2			712	137	75.6
700	93.7	88.5			826	158	87.8
800	93.9	88.7			941	180	99.7
900	94.0	89.0			1054	202	112
1000	94.2	89.3			1163	223	123
1250	94.5	89.8				276	153
1500	94.8	90.0				330	183
1750	95.0	90.0				383	212
2000	95.0	90.2				438	242
2250	95.0	90.5				491	272
2500	95.0	91.0				542	300
3000	95.0	91.5				647	358
3500	95.0	91.5				755	418

Source: G. L. Oscarson, *ABC of Large AC Motors and Control*, Machinery Manufacturing Co., 1973, Part 3, Controls, p. 15. Reprinted with permission.

would not be running simultaneously). Loads are turned on and off as needed, thus causing the system's power requirement to vary directly with the amount of on-line load. A system with varying load is said to be diversified.

Cyclic Operation

A daily load curve or profile for a typical system is shown in figure 3-5 where $p(t)$, the instantaneous value of load, is a function of time.

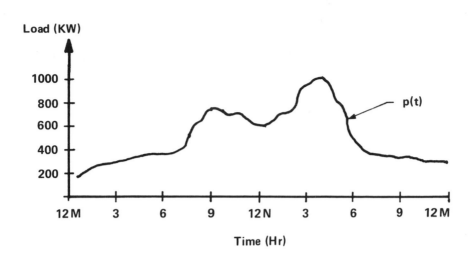

Figure 3-5. Load Profile of a Typical Composite Load System

The curve passes through peaks and valleys at various times of the day. For systems that utilize the same loads each day at about the same times, the curve tends to repeat its basic format every twenty-four hours. This cyclic operation is typical of many load systems due to such factors as life-style routines and production schemes. Cycle patterns may also exist with a period of a week, a month, or even a year depending on the individual cases. Some systems may exhibit little or no cyclic effects at all.

Energy Consumption

As power is fed to a load, energy is expended. Instantaneous power is defined as the rate at which electrical energy is consumed and is expressed by

$$p(t) = \frac{dw}{dt} .$$

(3.5)

Figure 3-6 illustrates a power function for a time interval t_0 to t_1 where time is in hours. The energy consumed during this interval is equal to the area under the curve. From equation (3.5) this energy is

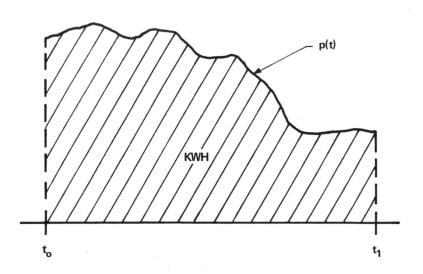

Figure 3-6. Energy Represented as the Area Under the Power Function

$$W = \int_{t_0}^{t_1} p(\tau) \; d\tau \qquad (3.6)$$

where W is the kilowatt-hours and τ is a dummy variable of integration. In general, active power is time-variant; however, for a steady load or constant power equation (3.6) reduces to

$$W = P \times (t_1 - t_0) \qquad (3.7)$$

where P is the value of the load in kilowatts.

For power company billing purposes the integration or summing of the energy is accomplished by a kilowatt-hour meter. The length of a typical billing cycle is thirty days or 720 hours.

Demand

Demand is the average value of load imposed on the electrical supply system over a period of time known as the *demand interval*. Figure 3-7 illustrates the demand of $p(t)$ for a demand interval of Δt. The average value of $p(t)$ is given by

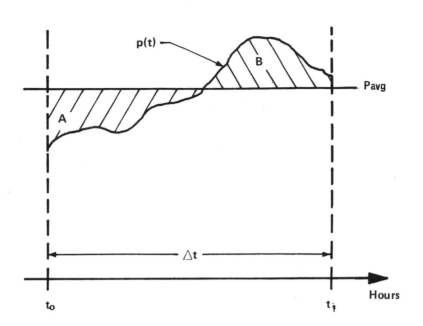

Figure 3-7. Demand and the Demand Interval

$$P_{avg} = \frac{1}{t_1 - t_0} \int_{t_0}^{t_1} p(\tau) \, d\tau \qquad (3.8)$$

where P_{avg} is the demand expressed in kilowatts.

As shown by figure 3-7, the area of the rectangle of height P_{avg} and width Δt is an approximation of the area under $p(t)$ between the limits of t_0 and t_1 (that is, area A is equal to area B). The demand is actually determined by dividing the kilowatt-hours accumulated during the demand interval by the length of the interval.

Since demand is an average, it will always be bounded by the highest and lowest values of the instantaneous load achieved during the demand interval (and equal to the load if the load is time-invariant during the interval). Therefore, if Δt were allowed to approach 0, the demand would approach the instantaneous load. Demand intervals vary among power companies, but commonly used values are fifteen, thirty, and sixty minutes.

Demand is figured consecutively during the billing cycle. For example, a billing period of thirty days or 720 hours with a demand interval of thirty minutes or 0.5 hour contains 1440 demand intervals and thus 1440 values of demand. The largest value of demand reached during the billing period is the *maximum demand*, which serves as the basis for the demand charge of the power bill.

The *demand factor* of a system is expressed as the ratio of maximum demand to the connected load. Normally the demand factor is less than unity and is equal to unity only if the connected load is operated at full load during a complete demand interval. The demand factor denotes the percentage of the connected load that is operated at one time.[16]

The *coincidence factor* is expressed as the ratio of the maximum demand of the composite load system to the sum of the maximum demands of the individual or component loads. This ratio equals unity only if the composite load demands occur at the same time. If these individual demands are not coincident, the system demand will be less than the sum of the composite load demands, and the ratio will be less than unity.[17] The inverse of the coincidence factor is the *diversity factor*, which, with the above conditions, has a value greater than or equal to unity.

Load Factor

Load factor is the ratio of the average load for a particular time interval to the peak load which is achieved during that interval. Either the maximum instantaneous load or the maximum demand may be used to express this peak value of load; however, maximum demand is often used for computing billing load factor. The load factor is usually determined by first dividing the kilowatt hours accumulated during a given period by the number of hours in that period to obtain the average load. The average load is then divided by the maximum demand to obtain the load factor given by

$$LF = \frac{KWH/Hrs}{KW\ Demand} = \frac{KW\ Average}{KW\ Demand}. \qquad (3.9)$$

Load factor may also be thought of as the ratio of the energy consumed during the period to the energy that could have been consumed during the period. From equation (3.9), this relationship is

$$LF = \frac{KWH}{(KW\ Demand) \times (Hrs)} \qquad (3.10)$$

where KWH is the actual kilowatt-hours. The product of the demand and the time of the period is the kilowatt-hours possible if the peak load had been sustained throughout the period.

Load factor denotes the extent to which the peak load is maintained during the interval under study. Load factor is typically calculated on a daily, weekly, monthly, or annual basis. When calculated for long time periods, the load factor is usually less than for short periods, since the average value of load generally decreases with longer averages and since the maximum demand remains the same or increases. The load factor of any constant and continuous load is 100 percent.

The *hours use of demand* is the ratio of kilowatt-hours accumulated during a time interval to the maximum load achieved during that same time. As with load factor, this ratio indicates the extent to which the peak load is sustained during the period.

Power Factor

All loads require active power or kilowatts to do useful work such as mechanical rotation. Loads that are reactive in nature also require reactive power or reactive kilovolt-amperes (RKVA) to do nonproductive work, such as providing the magnetic field for transformers and motors. As shown by figure 3-8, the active and reactive powers may be represented as vectors where the RKVA vector is in either positive or negative quadrature with the KW vector, depending on the impedance nature of the load.

The apparent power or kilovolt-amperes of the load is the resultant of the KW and RKVA vectors and is represented as a phasor whose magnitude and angle are given by

$$KVA = \sqrt{[(KW)^2 + (RKVA)^2]},$$

$$(3.11)$$

$$\text{and } \theta = \arctan(RKVA/KW).$$

Power factor is defined as the cosine of the angle θ. From equation (3.11), power factor may also be defined as the ratio of the real power to the apparent power as given by

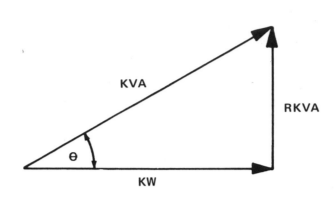

KVA

RKVA

θ

KW

Figure 3-8. Components of Power Represented as Vectors—The Power Triangle

$$PF = KW/KVA = \cos\theta . \qquad (3.12)$$

Since the cosine is a symmetrical function and θ is constrained to $-90 < \theta < 90$, the power factor will always be a positive value. By convention, a negative angle refers to a load having a net reactance that is inductive, in which case the load current lags the voltage by θ degrees; therefore, the corresponding power factor is said to be *lagging*. On the other hand, a positive angle refers to a net capacitive reactance, in which case the load current leads the voltage. In this case, the corresponding power factor is referred to as *leading*. A load containing only resistance has current and voltage in phase; therefore, θ equals 0, KVA equals KW, and the power factor is 1.0 or 100 percent.

Most loads tend to have a net reactance that is inductive and thus a lagging system power factor. The power factor usually varies throughout the load cycle, since the overall value is determined by the characteristics of the individual loads. The average value of power factor during a period of time can be determined from metering data, namely the kilowatt-hours and the reactive kilovolt-ampere hours accumulated during the period. The average power factor is given by

$$PF_{avg} = \cos\left[\arctan\left(RKVAH/KWH\right)\right] \qquad (3.13)$$

The power factor of a composite load is an indication of the degree to which the system capacity is being used efficiently. System efficiency is increased when the reactive power that must be supplied to the load by the generator is reduced. The benefits of power factor correction are discussed in chapters 5 and 6.

Summary

Loads are devices that transform electrical energy to other forms. Since losses are incurred in transformation, loads have an efficiency rating that is dependent on these losses. Loads may be categorized as lighting loads and power loads.

Individual loads operate together to form systems of composite loads. Although a composite load is unique, its characteristics are not completely unpredictable. The following chapter discusses energy surveying and methods of determining both individual and composite load characteristics.

4 Electrical Energy Auditing

The purpose of an energy survey or audit is to collect information systematically concerning the utilization of energy. The survey should attempt to document energy flows and the efficiency of energy use within the system. The results of the audit form an energy data base by which studies can be made and the effects of energy conservation management can be compared. The audit is essential to the effective application of conservation measures.

The topics discussed in this chapter include guidelines for conducting an electrical energy audit and means for determining various load characteristics. Suggested survey data forms and a checklist for analyzing audit data are presented.

Audit Guidelines

The audit is basically an accounting function. All values of power and energy should be expressed in a common unit; namely, kilowatts and kilowatt-hours. Other ratings, such as motor horsepower, should be converted to kilowatts, and the energy consumption estimated in kilowatt-hours. Often electricity is only a part of a system's energy sources; for example, fossil fuels are also common inputs. The basic unit most commonly used for considering "total energy" is the British thermal unit or Btu. Because of power plant efficiencies, approximately 10,000 Btu of fuel are burned by the electric utility to generate 1 kilowatt-hour (this value is referred to as the heat rate of a power plant); therefore, the "energy equivalent" for electric power is 10,000 Btu/KWH.[1] However, for the end-use calculations, 1 kilowatt-hour is equal to 3413 Btu.

The audit should include a study of both individual load performance and total system behavior. Actual energy use should be measured where possible and compared to the theoretical consumption. The variance between the actual and theoretical values is wasted energy and thus a target for energy management action.

45

Several surveys may be necessary to gather all of the pertinent information. Data ranging over long periods of time help to show trends in energy consumption and demand. Night and weekend surveys are of great importance, since large amounts of energy are often wasted during those times. Continuing surveys conducted throughout the year at regular intervals will show whether conservation efforts are profitable and will assist in keeping the data base up-to-date with system changes.

For large electrical systems, a significant manpower force may be necessary to conduct an accurate and useful audit. Surveys conducted by or in conjunction with departments or divisions of a company are generally best handled by using departmental personnel who have a familiarity with their particular systems. A central coordinating team can then organize the entire data for analysis.

Energy Audit Data Forms

To facilitate the systematic collection of energy data, an energy audit sheet or form should be developed. A format is needed for tabulating the load characteristics of the total system. These characteristics can be determined from past power bills, preferably over a multiyear period. Most bills have an energy charge for the kilowatt-hours that were consumed during each billing cycle. Other characteristics, such as power factor and demand, will appear on the bill only for those customers who have provisions for these characteristics in their rate contracts with the power company. The nature of the load will determine the rate structure and thus the complexity of the metering installation required. A suggested energy audit data form for the collection of such data is illustrated in figure 4-1.

Tabulation of charges from each bill is helpful in determining economic trends with regard to price changes in energy and fuel adjustment costs. A copy of the rate structure should be included with the audit form so that economic studies can be made.

A format is also needed for surveying individual loads. The general characteristics that should be considered are

1. Nameplate rating in kilowatts or kilovolt-amperes,
2. Operating voltage,
3. Load current,

Company: _____ Location: _____

Type of Business: _____ Prepared by: _____ Date: _____

Year:	Energy		Demand		Fuel Adjustment	Total Cost	Cost per KWH	Load Factor	Power Factor
	Kilowatt-hours	Cost	KW or KVA	Cost					
Jan.									
Feb.									
Mar.									
Apr.									
May									
June									
July									
Aug.									
Sept.									
Oct.									
Nov.									
Dec.									
Total									

Figure 4-1. Suggested Energy Audit Form

4. Power factor,
5. Efficiency, and
6. Hours of operation on a daily, weekly, or monthly basis.

Not all of these characteristics are pertinent to every load, and some of the characteristics may have to be determined by estimation and/or measurements. For example, the kilowatt rating of a motor may be estimated from the horsepower rating; the kilovolt-amperes can then be determined by measuring the voltage and current and taking the product of the two. Some of the characteristics can be calculated from other known characteristics. For instance, the ratio of KW to KVA from the example presented here gives the power factor of the motor.

The power requirements of a load in kilowatts multiplied by its monthly operating hours is the energy a device consumes in a month. If accurate estimates of monthly consumption of the primary loads can be made, comparison to the power bill will yield the percentage of the total energy consumed by each device and thus the energy flows in the system.

A suggested load survey sheet is presented in figure 4-2. Data that are not easily attainable should be estimated as accurately as possible. Other useful factors, such as whether a device operates during a system peak period, should also be noted on the survey sheet.

Checklist

Before surveying the electrical loads, a checklist should be devised to be used in the audit to help indicate "hidden" energy wasters. Such a list might include

1. Employee energy use habits,
2. Maintenance records,
3. Over-sized and/or excessively used lights and equipment,
4. Circuit loads on primary and secondary feeders,
5. Waste heat from industrial processes, and
6. Insulation of structures, furnaces, and ducts.

As the survey is being conducted, suggestions for energy management action should be noted and submitted for analysis. Chapter 6

ELECTRICAL LOAD SURVEY FORM

Company: _____   Location: _____

Type of Business: _____   Prepared by: _____   Date: _____

Item Description	Rating		Operating:		Power Factor	Efficiency	Hours of Use			Special Notes
	KW	KVA	Voltage	Current			Day	Wk	Mo	

Figure 4-2. Suggested Load Survey Form

investigates some of the various conservation programs that can be administered in light of these items.

Determination of Load Characteristics

The power company's metering equipment at the service entrance provides data about the total system load. A simple kilowatt-hour meter can be used to determine the average load over any desired interval of time by counting the number of revolutions of the meter disk during that interval. The average load is then given by

$$P_{avg} = (k_h \times PT \times CT \times R \times 3.6)/t \qquad (4.1)$$

where k_h is the meter disk constant in watt-hours per revolution, PT is the potential transformer ratio, CT is the current transformer ratio, and R is the number of revolutions of the disk during t seconds. The PT and CT ratios are equal to 1 if the metering installation is self-contained—for example, residential.

For large customers, the power company's metering installation usually contains a device which records data. Included with the kilowatt-hour (KWH) meter are a reactive kilovolt-ampere-hour (RKVAH) meter and a device for determining time (that is, the demand interval). Information such as KW or KVA demand is recorded on strip or circular paper charts; or KWH, RKVAH, and time pulses from the meters are recorded on magnetic or punched tape. These tapes must then be run through an interpreter to obtain a printout of demand, power factor (PF), etc. Sometimes power companies can provide extensive data for customer use.

Portable recording meters, which print profiles of current, voltage, etc., against time on paper strip charts, can be used to monitor individual loads. Various meters are available for this type of survey, including

1. Voltmeters,
2. Ammeters,
3. Wattmeters,
4. Volt-ampere meters,
5. Reactive volt-ampere meters, and
6. Power factor meters.

By running the proper combinations of these meters and then synchronizing the strip charts, other information may be derived. For example, a KVA and a PF meter can be used to determine the corresponding values of KW and RKVA.

It is best if the meters are operated for at least one billing cycle. If plant operation varies significantly each month, the meters should be operated over a longer period of time. Meters for the survey may be bought or rented.

Audit Recap and Study

After all audit data has been gathered, the data should be analyzed in terms of the following questions:[2]

Total System Load

1. What were the maximum and minimum values of load? When did they occur? How long were they sustained?
2. How do the maximum and minimum loads compare to the average load (that is, load factor)?
3. Do maximum and minimum loads recur on a daily, weekly, or monthly basis? When these maximum and minimum loads occur, do they generally occur at the same time of the day?
4. How quickly does the system rise to (and fall from) full operating load?
5. What are the maximum, minimum, and average values of power factor, and when do the extreme values occur?
6. What is the nature of the load during lunch periods, nights, and weekends?

Individual Loads

1. What are the equipment maximum and minimum (or idle) values of the load?
2. Does the equipment operate during a system peak load period?
3. Do similar machines produce compatible load values?
4. Has the equipment been operating according to routine schedules?
5. Have equipment load measurements changed since previous surveys?
6. Are feeder circuit voltages within allowable tolerances?

Additional information should be gathered with system modifications and expansions, and spot checks should be made periodically to keep the survey records up-to-date.

Summary

The energy audit is essential in understanding the energy consumption and utilization characteristics of the load system. Individual and composite load data are collected systematically for analysis. The audit then serves as a basis for designing energy management programs and measuring their effects. Without the audit, accurate energy savings could not be computed.

The following chapter presents various load management techniques that modify system energy consumption patterns. Energy use modifications may be initiated by the customer, the utility, or both.

Load Management Techniques

Load management is the process of scheduling load usage so as to reduce electric energy consumption during peak load periods. This process suggests an increase in off-peak energy consumption. The goal of any load management program is to maintain, as nearly as possible, a constant level of load, thereby allowing the system load factor to approach 100 percent.

Various load management practices of electric power utilities are presented in this chapter. Customer use of electrical load controllers for demand-limiting purposes is also discussed.

Benefits of Load Management

Load management techniques have been utilized for quite a few years; however, in light of the energy crisis, interest in load management as an economical conservation measure has increased. Such programs offer several benefits[1] to the whole electric energy system. Reduced demand for electricity provides the capacity for load growth on the existing system. Large-scale load management schemes may delay the immediate need for new generating stations and/or upgraded network facilities.

An increase in load factor allows for a more efficient operation of generation, transmission, and distribution plants and thus a more equitable utilization of the capital investment. A reduction of energy consumption during heavy load periods lessens the requirements for "peaking" generation units that are less efficient and more costly to operate than "base load" generation plants.

Demand Control

Methods of load or demand control are utilized to "shave" or limit peak power. Demand control can be effected by three basic methods, namely

1. Timed control,
2. Manual control, and
3. Centralized control.

   The timed control method switches loads off and on according to a continuous cycle based on an estimate of peak load times. This type of control has no input concerning the rate of energy consumption by the load system; therefore, the effectiveness of timed control depends on a consistent cyclic energy consumption pattern.

   The manual control method is dependent on human decision-making ability. An operator monitors a demand meter throughout all demand intervals that occur during peak load periods and determines when to turn off and on selective loads to prevent the system demand from exceeding a predetermined limit. The accuracy of this method decreases with an increasing number of loads to control.

   Systems having many loads are best controlled by electronic instrumentation, such as hardwired controllers and minicomputers. Centralized control devices monitor system energy consumption and/or demand and "decide" when available loads should be turned off or on.

Load Shedding and Restoring

The process of turning loads off and on is referred to as *load shedding* and *restoring*. The total possible shedding ability of a system is given by

$$\text{LSP} = \frac{1}{\Delta t} \sum_{i=1}^{n} (L_i \times t_{\text{off}}) \qquad (5.1)$$

where LSP is the load shed potential in kilowatts, Δt is the demand interval in minutes, L_i is the load kilowatts under consideration for shedding, and t_{off} is the allowable off-time in minutes during the demand interval of the L_i load. The LSP represents the maximum possible reduction in demand for the electric system through load shedding.

   Loads which are shed are later restored (that is, after t_{off} is exceeded). Restored loads are either recoverable as with air conditioners or non-recoverable as with ventilation fans. A large or extra amount of the kilowatt-hours saved during the shed time of a recoverable load might be consumed after the load is restored to recover a nominal operating level. In this case no energy is conserved; however, the deferral of energy consumption from a peak load period to an off-peak period reduces demand, thus improving load factor. A nonrecoverable load, on the other hand, not only lowers demand but also consumes no extra kilowatt-hours to regain a status prior to the shed.[2]

Typical electrical loads that can be considered for load shedding/restoring operations are

1. Arc furnaces,
2. Battery chargers,
3. Chillers,
4. Circulating fans,
5. Compressors,
6. Exhaust fans,
7. Furnaces,
8. Grinders,
9. HVAC equipment,
10. Incinerators,
11. Intake fans,
12. Lighting,
13. Paper shredders,
14. Pool-heaters,
15. Pumps,
16. Small motors,
17. Snow melters,
18. Space heaters,
19. Tank agitators,
20. Trash compactors, and
21. Water heaters.

Loads should be studied in light of any harmful effects that could result due to load-shedding operations. Generally, large motors should not be considered for shedding applications because of large inrush starting currents and start/stop stresses. Loads that must operate constantly or on a definite schedule are referred to as *base loads* and are ineligible for shedding. Base loads normally include most production and life-safety equipment.

Some production loads may be classified as limited control loads since these loads are usually only shed in special situations. For example, the Diamond Match Division of the Diamond International Corporation at Cloquet, Minnesota, applied demand control to a saw and a log debarking machine. Because the output of these machines was in excess of the normal production rate, operations could be easily shut down for a few minutes to reduce demand without creating idle labor.[3]

System Operation

Centralized demand control systems require some manner of data acquisition so that energy consumption and/or demand can be monitored. With many control systems, signals are obtained from the power company's metering installation. Meters equipped with pulse initiation devices are used to provide KWH (and in special cases RKVAH) pulses to the customer. Some systems also require an end-of-demand interval (EOI) pulse for synchronization with the power company's demand interval.[4] Power companies often require the installation of isolation relays between the meters and the customer's attachment point to prevent interference between systems.

The goal of centralized control is to limit demand by shaving the peaks and filling in the valleys of the power curve. The power then approaches a constant level. The desired demand is sometimes termed the *target demand*.[5] Once a target is selected, the ideal quantity of KWH pulses necessary during the demand interval to yield that target is given by

$$P_{td} = \frac{TD \times \Delta t}{0.001 \times K_h} \tag{5.2}$$

where P_{td} is the number of pulses, TD is the target demand in KW, Δt is the demand interval in hours, and K_h is the meter constant in watt-hours/pulse.

For a steady-state load, pulses are accumulated at a rate given by

$$R = \frac{P_{td}}{3600 \times \Delta t} \text{ pulses/sec} \tag{5.3}$$

where R is the slope of the line representing the ideal rate of energy consumption in figure 5-1. On the other hand, a time variant system of loads (the actual case in application) has a consumption rate that varies. The three basic techniques of load control are based on the rate of energy consumption. These techniques are the

1. Ideal rate method,
2. Instantaneous rate method, and
3. True forecast method.

Ideal Rate Method. The ideal rate method of load control is illustrated in figure 5-2. The ideal rate line from figure 5-1 has been modified by an offset number of pulses which represent that fraction of the full load capable of load shed control.[6] The offset pulses (P_{os}) are given by

$$P_{os} = P_{td} \times \frac{\text{Controllable KW}}{\text{Connected KW}} . \tag{5.4}$$

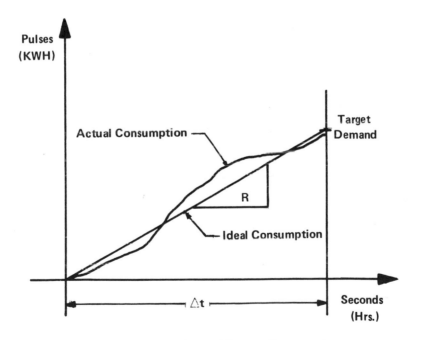

Figure 5-1. Ideal Rate of Energy Consumption

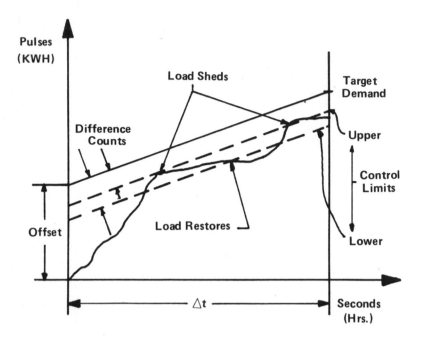

Figure 5-2. Ideal Rate Method of Load Control

The offset provides a buffer against premature load control early in the demand interval.

Located below and parallel to the modified ideal rate curve are the upper and lower control limits. An up-down counter is used to compare the actual usage rate with the ideal rate that is generated internally. When the difference count between the ideal and actual pulses reaches the upper control limit, loads are shed on a priority basis. Shedding of all available loads will continue above the upper control limit. When the difference drops to the lower control limit, loads are restored. At the end of each demand interval, the EOI signal is received from either the utility's metering unit or from an internal clock that is synchronized with the utility's demand interval. Any loads that have not been restored by the EOI pulse are added at the beginning of the next demand interval.

Instantaneous Rate Method. As with the ideal rate method, the instantaneous rate method of control is based on the comparison of the actual energy consumption rate to a preset ideal rate. As

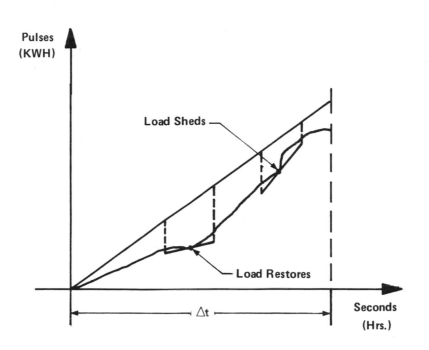

Figure 5-3. Instantaneous Rate Method of Load Control

illustrated by figure 5-3, the criterion for load control action is based on the instantaneous slope (rate) of the actual consumption curve. When the actual pulse rate exceeds the ideal rate, loads are shed. When the actual pulse rate drops below the ideal rate, loads are restored. Limits are set for shed/restore operation to prevent continuous on-and-off cycling when the power level is fairly constant.

This technique of control requires no EOI pulse, as the demand interval is only relevant for the calculation of the ideal rate (equation 4.3). Current and potential transformers can be used to provide an input if pulses are unavailable from the utility's metering installation.

True Forecast Method. The true forecast method of control is normally accomplished by a computer and is most effective with large load centers. As illustrated by figure 5-4, the computer accumulates the KWH pulses throughout the demand interval and calculates the rate at which the pulses are received. The demand interval is partitioned into several forecast intervals. The rate of

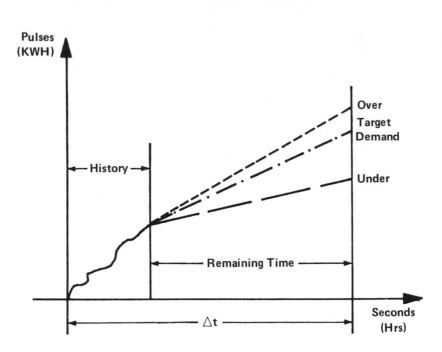

Figure 5-4. True Forecast Method of Load Control

energy consumption is computed at each forecast interval, and a straight-line approximation is made to estimate (or forecast) the final number of pulses to be accumulated by the end of the demand interval. The forecast estimate[7] in pulses is given by

Pulse Forecast = Pulses Accumulated

+ (Current Pulse Rate × Remaining Time). (5.5)

The forecast is compared to the target demand. If the forecast indicates that the target will be exceeded (forecast: over), loads are shed. If the forecast is less than the target (forecast: under), loads are restored. Unlike the ideal rate method, control action may take place early in the demand interval.

Electric Utility Practices

Electric utilities are showing an increasing interest in the application of load management as an economical means of improving the efficiency of the electric energy system. Utilities are also educating and motivating their customers in the development of load management schemes. The cooperation of both parties is necessary for an effective program.

Some power companies' load management efforts are not directly sensed by the consumers. For instance, off-peak pumping and storage of water at hydroelectric generating stations for use during peak load periods is a common procedure. Although this practice is directly beneficial to the power company, there is no impact from the consumers' point of view.[8] On the other hand, rate structure modifications or energy rationing could greatly affect consumer life styles.

As a representative example of the electric power industry's interest in utility-consumer load management activities, Public Service Company of Indiana, Inc., is administering the following program.[9] Public Service is urging customers of all classes to increase their end use efficiency of electrical energy consumption. The program is designed to educate consumers about such topics as energy efficiency ratios (EER) and power demand management (PDM). System customers are encouraged to increase load factor by utilizing conventional off-peak loads (for example, outdoor lighting) and by delaying peak period energy consumption to off-peak periods. Programs of this nature encourage load management in both the business and private communities. Many utility load management programs are of significant size and investment.

Control of Customer Loads

Power companies are capable of employing centralized control on a large-scale basis. The load shed/restore operations are analogous to the methods previously discussed; however, control signals must be transmitted to the load sites from a centralized control point, such as a distribution substation. Three types of channels may be used for information transmission. These channels are

1. Communication wires,
2. Radio frequency transmission, and
3. Power distribution and/or transmission network conductors.

Generally, communication lines are too expensive to install and maintain; however, their use may be favorable in specialized cases.

The most common control methods are accomplished by radio control (using radio frequency transmission) and ripple control (using power system conductors).

Radio Control. A radio control system requires (a) a transmitter at a centralized point and (b) a receiver, a control device for each load, and a separate meter for the controllable loads at the load site. Coded signals discriminate between loads to be controlled. This method is somewhat bounded by the limited number of available frequencies.

Radio control of residential water heaters has been utilized for several years. Experimental control of other loads is currently being investigated by various utilities. For example, the Detroit Edison Company conducted a pilot program to control fifty residential air conditioning systems during the summer of 1975.[10] The units were shed for ten to twenty minutes each hour for no longer than five hours in succession. The customers realized no significant difference in comfort as a result of the reduced use of the air conditioning. Billing credits were based on the size of the units that were metered separately from the rest of the residential loads.

Ripple Control. The ripple control or "centralized network control" method utilizes the conductors that supply power to a load as a channel for the control information. Audio frequency sine wave signals (thus the term *ripple control*) are injected into the electric network by means of a coupling circuit typically located at a substation. A programmable unit is used to initiate the control signals at the proper times. The signals are received and processed at the load sites. Noncontrollable equipment connected to the system are unaffected by the signals.

Ripple control has been utilized intensely in Europe and is currently in the experimental stage by a few American power companies. The Central Vermont Public Service Corporation (CVPS) recently installed a ripple control system for a two year study.[11] Approximately 200 CVPS customers will allow common household appliances such as clothes washers and dryers, electric water heaters, and freezers to be controlled by the system. Ripple control equipment also has the capability to control power system devices such as transformer load tap changers (LTC) and capacitor banks.

Capacitor Application

Capacitors are installed at substations and on primary distribution feeder circuits to correct low power factor. Power capacitors are typically rated in units of cKVAR (same as RKVA). "Fixed" capacitors having a value of capacitive cKVAR equal to the minimum inductive KVAR load of the circuit are operated continuously. "Switched" capacitors are energized only during peak load periods to prevent a leading power factor during off-peak periods.

Capacitor installations release substation and generation capacity (apparent power), thus allowing room for load growth without drastic upgrading of equipment. The released capacity is given by

$$\Delta KVA = \sqrt{[(KVA)^2 - (cKVAR \cos \theta)^2]} + (cKVAR \sin \theta) - KVA$$

$$(5.6)$$

where ΔKVA is the released capacity, KVA is the capacity of either the substation or the generator, cKVAR is the rating of the installed capacitors, and θ is the uncorrected power factor angle. Feeder circuit capacity is similarly released, as given by

$$\Delta KVA = \frac{X(cKVAR)}{X(\sin \theta) + R(\cos \theta)} \qquad (5.7)$$

where R and X are the per phase values of resistance and reactance of the line.

Capacitors also improve voltage on a line. Since capacitor current flows toward the source (substation), a cancellation effect occurs with the inductive load current and the total or apparent current is reduced. The normal voltage drop along the line is therefore reduced (or conversely, a voltage rise occurs). The percentage voltage rise is the product of the capacitor current and the circuit reactance between the substation bus and the capacitor, as given by

$$\%V_{rise} = \frac{cKVAR}{10 \times (KV)^2} \times X \qquad (5.8)$$

where KV is the line-to-line voltage if the cKVAR rating is three phase and line-to-neutral voltage if the rating is single phase.

Capacitors are most beneficial when installed at each load site; however, for feeders with various load distributions, capacitor banks are generally located at a point where the inductive load KVAR is equal to one-half the capacitor cKVAR. The technical and economic benefits of capacitors are further discussed in chapter 6.

Incentive Rate Structure

Campàigns are necessary to educate consumers as to how and why load management should be applied. Many utilities are marketing load management by urging their customers to delay energy usage until off-peak hours. The success of this method depends on the consumer's desire and ability to alter present life styles.

Experiments in "time-of-day metering" are being conducted by various power companies. This strategy, also referred to as peak-load-pricing, is basically a dual rate structure in which energy consumption costs are cheaper during off-peak periods (typically nighttime hours) than during peak load periods. Thus the incentive to modify energy use patterns is induced in the consumer. Peak-load-pricing metering installations require meters having dual KWH consumption registers for the two periods. Switching between registers can be accomplished by time controls or by ripple control techniques.

Curtailable service rates are also used as a load management practice, particularly with large industries. Service contracts of this nature are feasible for customers having alternate sources of power and/or production operations that are compatible with curtailment procedures. This method of load management is often preferable to energy rationing methods, as most curtailments are short-term in nature.

In the opinion of Dr. Bruce L. Jaffee, assistant professor of business economics and public policy at Indiana University, three general types of reforms[1,2] are expected to develop in the next few years due to pressure from environmental and public interest movements. These reforms, listed here, could affect consumer use of electricity.

1. The declining block structure, typical to many rate schedules, might be flattened or completely banished (also referred to as levelized rates) on the grounds that energy use is currently

promoted through decreasing prices for increasing quantities of consumption.

2. Peak load (time-of-day) pricing could occur to make the peak load period energy consumers obligated to supply revenue to help cover any system upgrading costs necessary to ensure reliable peak service.

3. An incorporation of environmental-related costs in the rate schedule to aid the utility in meeting high-level expenditures imposed by pollution control regulations may also result (thereby allowing the combustion of cheaper fuels).

Voltage Reduction

Voltage reduction is occasionally used as a load management technique, particularly when the generation capacity approaches an insufficient level (low level of spinning reserve or standby capacity) for supplying reliable service during peak periods. Voltage reduction lowers power flow; however, as shown by table 5-1, undervoltage may have inefficient or even harmful effects on various utilization equipment.

Transformer and Feeder Load Management

The purpose of a transformer load management (TLM) program is to optimize economically the use of distribution transformer capacity. The TLM program is based on a mathematical relationship between KVA and KWH. Various relationships may be derived depending on the criteria and assumptions used in the development.

The Baltimore Gas and Electric Company has designed a TLM system that incorporates a rather unique feature. The system normally issues an assessment of peak loading (demand) on all distribution transformers under consideration. In addition, the TLM system also produces operating instructions for the most economical utilization of each transformer. These instructions include (a) replacing a transformer with a transformer at the appropriate capacity (either smaller or larger), (b) testing the transformer, or (c) leaving the transformer in place. A computer program is used to make the analysis for recommendation. Costs incurred by transformer regulation, power

Table 5-1
Typical Effects of Undervoltage on Utilization Equipment

Induction motors	10 percent undervoltage decreases starting and maximum running torque 19 percent, decreases full load speed 1 1/2 percent, increases full load current 11 percent, and causes a slight rise in operating temperature.
Incandescent lamps	10 percent undervoltage reduces light output 30 percent; 20 percent undervoltage reduces light output over 50 percent.
Flourescent lamps	10 percent undervoltage cuts light output about 10 percent. Low voltage often results in unsatisfactory starting.
HID lamps	10 percent undervoltage reduces mercury vapor light output 15 percent to 25 percent and other types 5 percent to 15 percent, depending on ballast type. There may also be a color shift. Lamps go out at 15 percent to 20 percent undervoltage.
Resistance heaters	10 percent undervoltage produces a 19 percent decrease in heat output.
Infrared heating	Radiant energy is nearly proportional to wattage. Undervoltage lengthens processing time, decreases production.
Electronic equipment	Undervoltage drastically reduces tube life and can destroy gas-filled tubes in minutes.
Capacitors	The corrective capacity varies with the square of the voltage; 10 percent undervoltage reduces corrective capacity almost 20 percent.

Source: "Getting Power From Here to There Efficiently," *Electrified Industry* 39 (July 1975): 7. Reprinted with permission.

losses (core and copper losses), change-outs, carrying charges on investment, and outages are included in the economic analysis.[13]

The technology gain from TLM programs is being used to develop a higher order system referred to as feeder load management (FLM). The Dallas Power and Light Company has designed an FLM system that will furnish analysis reports on every distribution circuit. Typical information provided by the report includes available fault currents, feeder voltage profiles, and circuit loading. The program will also be useful for balancing three-phase loads on primary circuits and providing accurate data for voltage regulator and capacitor applications.[14]

TLM and FLM systems greatly increase the efficiency of the electric energy system. The future use of these programs will be invaluable to both the planning and the operating personnel of the utility industry. Guesswork will be replaced by a continually increasing data base from which accurate engineering can be accomplished.

Impediments to Load Management

Studies should be made to determine what effects will occur as a result of load management action. For instance, *some* demand control systems shed significant amounts of load only during the last few minutes of each demand interval. The load is then restored at the beginning of the next interval. Large cycling loads of this nature could impose serious operating problems on the utility's system.

Another demand control problem is that of "peak splitting." In this case a peak load is split between two adjacent demand intervals. Although the average metered load for each interval is less than if the peak load had occurred during a single interval, the actual thermal loading (which actually determines capacity) on the system is unchanged. The power company thus loses revenue needed for recovering the cost of the peak load capacity equipment necessary for reliable service.

As stated previously, a sense of general understanding and cooperation between the utility and the consumer is necessary for load management to be practical. Proposed load management activities should be communicated to all parties involved. A joint effort could help to stabilize the escalating costs of electric energy.

Summary

Load management is the process of shaping electrical energy use patterns so as to optimize the performance of the electric energy system. By shifting energy consumption from peak load periods to off-peak periods, a more constant level of power can be maintained.

Electric utilities implement large-scale load management programs to increase system load factor. Consumers also initiate load management (for example, demand control) as an energy conservation measure. The economic benefits of various load management programs as well as other energy conservation management programs are discussed in the following chapter.

6

**Electrical Energy
Management Program
Design**

In chapter 4, information was given on how energy audit data should
be collected. This data should be analyzed to determine (a) where
energy is being wasted and (b) how much energy is being wasted. The
effects of various electrical energy management programs can then be
studied so that potential money and energy savings can be estimated.
Those programs which are found to be economically feasible can
then be implemented.

This chapter cites some of the reasons for energy waste within
building electrical systems. Various electrical energy conservation
programs are presented to illustrate some of the potential areas for
energy savings. A preliminary financial analysis procedure is offered
as a means of estimating the potential profitability of alternative
programs.

Building Systems and Equipment Inefficiencies

Inefficiencies of electrical equipment installations in older buildings
generally occur because of two factors. First, the design philosophy
of the building was based on an abundance of cheap energy sources.
As a result, little attention was given to energy conservation. Second,
electrical system changes and expansions during the intervening
period usually have been accomplished without upgrading the total
system. As a result, existing buildings and equipment that were
constructed at a low first cost now often have high operating costs
due to low operating efficiencies.

Electrical equipment such as motors and transformers normally
operate with optimum efficiencies at rated load. If a motor is
oversized for its task, more load current is utilized than necessary. If
a motor is undersized for its task, the motor's life is decreased
because of the thermal stresses placed on the motor. If load has
increased significantly in a system, transformers may, for example,
be overloaded beyond their thermal limits, thus causing low voltage,
reduced life, and the potential for an outage.

The current carrying capability (ampacity) of the electrical circuits may also be exceeded as a result of load growth. As current increases, voltage drop and power losses similarly increase. Loose connections and short circuits draw excessive currents, which present both energy wastes and safety hazards.

Other building systems, such as lighting and comfort conditioning equipment, are often found to be energy wasters. The lumen output of an electric lamp decreases with time; therefore, the lighting system operates more efficiently if bulb replacement is made before burnout occurs. The HVAC system is usually the largest energy-consuming component in all buildings. Improper insulation levels may account for excessive operation of HVAC equipment.

Man-Made Inefficiencies

Large amounts of energy waste may be attributed to life styles. Some business employees tend to be less energy-conservation-minded, since power bills are paid by the company. For example, lights and machines are often left energized continuously (thus increasing the system base load), whereas intermittent operation would suffice. The cheap energy habits of the past are often difficult to alter now.

Industrial production schedules determine the basic load pattern of a plant. Typically, load peaks are generated in the morning and afternoon. Quick start-up and shutdown operations may reduce load factor. Bulk load changes of this nature often impose difficulties to the economical supply of power.

System efficiency declines with time—for example, filters become dirty and drive belts become worn. The lack of a regular maintenance routine results not only in additional energy costs but also in the reduced life of equipment. Often maintenance work is not authorized until a problem exists. On the other hand, a planned preventative maintenance program helps to keep system efficiency at optimum levels.

Analysis for Potential Energy Savings

Several electrical energy management programs are presented here. Methods for estimating potential money and energy savings are developed where possible. Programs may be selected according to company needs and investment policies.

Education Programs

The first energy management project that should be undertaken by a business is that of educating people about the energy crisis. Employees should be informed of the company's particular energy problems. Literature, films, and discussions are effective in motivating employees to become conservation-minded both on the job and at home.

Employees should be instructed as to how they can conserve energy. Special instructions and reminders should be posted. The personnel who will directly assist in implementing particular conservation programs should be given special training. Invited suggestions from employees are effective means of realizing more conservation opportunities.

Many businesses are encouraging their customers and the communities which they serve to practice energy conservation. For instance, some public utilities include with the monthly bill a small newsletter addressing energy problems and methods of conservation. Programs of this nature help to maintain good public relations.

Load Cycle Rescheduling Programs

A review of load operation schemes may reveal that certain equipment may be rescheduled to operate at other times without affecting production output. In this manner, selective loads may be shifted from peak load to off-peak load periods to reduce demand. However, the shifting of loads does not reduce the total energy consumption, since the duration of operating time is unchanged.

The following example[1] illustrates the annual savings realized by the rescheduling of a load. A municipal water company operates a 500 horsepower motor load during the day work shift. The electric company, which utilizes time-of-day metering, offers a monthly rate reduction in demand charges of $1.50 per kilowatt demand if the load is operated during the late night shift. The annual savings due to the rescheduling of this motor can be estimated in the following manner.

$$\text{Annual Savings} = 500 \text{ hp} \times 0.766 \text{ KW/hp}$$
$$\times \ \$1.50/\text{KW/mo} \times 12 \text{ mo/yr}$$
$$= \underline{\$6,894.00}$$

Although not all power companies offer off-peak rates, any load reduction during peak periods will reduce demand.

The flexibility to alter equipment operation schedules varies with the types of processes and equipment involved and the number of daily work shifts. A plot of the daily load cycle will aid in the determination of peak and off-peak load periods.

Maintenance Programs

As stated earlier, a preventative maintenance program is an effective means of optimizing system efficiency. A total maintenance routine could consist of several time frames for inspection and action, namely

1. Weekly,
2. Monthly,
3. Quarterly or seasonally,
4. Semiannually,
5. Annually, and
6. During emergency conditions.

Maintenance schedules vary with the environment. For instance, a piece of equipment situated in a production environment may require more frequent maintenance than the same piece of equipment situated in a business office atmosphere.

Motors. Motors constitute a large percentage of the load within buildings and plants. A suggested general maintenance program checklist,[2] based on an eight-hour day, for motors and associated equipment is given here. (Since this checklist is general in nature, motor size, type, and application will dictate the appropriate maintenance actions.)

Weekly:

    Motors—lubricate; check brushes; clean

    Motor Controls—check breakers

Quarterly:

    Motor Controls—clean contacts and mechanism; check coils, magnets, and connections, lubricate (if applies)

Semiannually:

    Motors—lubricate; check speed, alignment, commutator, brushes, and tightness

    Gear Motors and Speed Reducers—lubricate; check alignment

Annually:

    Motors—overhaul; test insulation; check rotor clearances, commutator, connections, and load

Motor manufacturers should be consulted as to specific maintenance schemes.

Comfort Conditioning Systems. HVAC equipment include not only the air treatment plant and distribution system but also the associated controls. Regular maintenance inspections should include air filters, belt and drive systems, and thermostats. Since HVAC equipment vary in design, a specific maintenance routine should be developed for a particular system. As with motor maintenance, HVAC manufacturers should be consulted for maintenance procedures for their equipment.

Lighting. Lighting maintenance consists primarily of cleaning and replacement. Cleaning intervals are determined by the lamp locations (for example, less dust accumulation in an office than in a factory). Proper fixture ventilation reduces dirt buildup. Cleaning includes not only the lamp and fixtures but also the reflecting surfaces of the room. Use of light-colored paint on the ceiling and walls increases the reflective properties of the room.

Lamp replacement intervals depend on the hours of use of the lamps. Light output decreases with time due to lumen depreciation; therefore, replacement according to hours use, rather than at burnout, is most efficient. Lamp "mortality" characteristics for determining replacement intervals can be obtained from manufacturers.

The replacement of individual lamps at burnout is referred to as *spot replacement;* whereas replacement of the total lighting system at one time is referred to as *group relamping.* With group relamping, bulbs will be replaced that are still capable of delivering an acceptable amount of light. These lamps may be retained for use as interim replacements between group relamping intervals.

The costs for spot and group replacement schemes are computed by the following equations:[3]

Spot lamp replacement:

$$C_s = P + L_s .$$ (6.1)

Group lamp replacement including interim replacement:

$$C_g = [P + L_g + (B \times L_s)]/I .$$ (6.2)

In these equations C_s and C_g are the total replacement costs per lamp for spot and group replacement, respectively; P is the price of a single lamp; L_s is the labor cost per lamp for spot replacement; L_g is the labor cost per lamp for group replacement; B is the ratio of burned-out lamps to total lamps for the group relamping interval; and I is the ratio of the group relamping interval to the average lamp life. Should analysis show that the costs for spot replacement versus group relamping are equal, group relamping has the added advantage of more light delivered, better appearance, and fewer work interruptions.[4]

Equipment Replacement Programs

Equipment replacements for energy savings may be accomplished either (a) by allowing an existing device to remain in service until the end of its rated life and then replacing the device with a new, more efficient model or (b) by immediately substituting a more efficient device before the end of its rated life. A detailed analysis involving the purchase, installation, and operating costs may be necessary to justify the choice between (a) or (b).

An example of case (a) might be the consideration of the replacement of an immersion element boiler, which is nearing the end of its rated life, with a more efficient electrode boiler. Suppose that an analysis reveals (1) that a need for increased capacity is unnecessary before the end of the boiler's life span and (2) that an investment in an electrode boiler at this time could not approach the economic advantage which the investments could gain if it were allocated to another project. Investment in the electrode boiler could then be delayed until the immersion element boiler reached the end of its rated life.

An example of case (b) might be the consideration of replacing an oversized motor with a smaller motor more suited to the task. Suppose that an analysis shows that with the savings realized through reduced load current, the capital investment for the smaller motor could be recovered within an acceptable time period. The investment for the smaller motor could then be made, and the larger motor could be sold at a salvage price or retained in stock for a more suitable task.

The energy audit may reveal inefficient loads that may be candidates for replacement. Service upgrading through increased feeder capacity should also be considered. Reconductoring of overloaded circuits with higher ampacity wire reduces voltage drop and power losses and allows for future load growth. Increased transformer capacity might also be necessary. High voltage levels are most efficient; however, the number of voltage transformations necessary to serve the loads should be minimized.

Energy Reduction Device Programs

Large-scale energy management programs may include significant investments for equipment whose primary purpose is to reduce system energy consumption by large quantities. A careful review of system operation and performance is necessary to select such equipment.

Capacitors. Capacitors are used to correct poor or low power factor in a system. The value of power factor that the system should economically be corrected to is determined by

$$PF_e = \sqrt{[1 - (C/S)^2]} \qquad (6.3)$$

where PF_e is the economical power factor, C is the installed cost per RKVA of the capacitors, and S is the cost per KVA of the system. The RKVA value of capacitors needed to correct to the economical power factor is given by

$$RKVA = PF_o \times L_p \times M \qquad (6.4)$$

where PF_o is the original power factor, L_p is the peak load in KVA, and M is the KW correction multiplier from table 6-1. For example, to correct an original power factor of 75 percent to a power factor of 95 percent, the proper correction multiplier from table 6-1 is 0.553.

Fixed capacitors, equal to the minimum inductive kilovars of the system, are installed to correct power factor during off-peak conditions; whereas switched capacitors are installed but only operate during peak load periods (to prevent leading power factor). Switched capacitors are often located near motor centers and are simultaneously operated with the motors. Switched capacitors are also operated by various control devices, including

1. Voltage controls,
2. Current controls,
3. Time controls,
4. Power factor controls, and
5. Temperature controls.

Capacitors installed at the load site reduce energy losses in the supply conductors (since load current is reduced). However, monetary savings will be realized only if the power factor is a "billing" variable stipulated in the electric rate contract. Annual savings can be estimated by recalculating the past twelve months power bills using the new value of power factor (PF_e).

Centralized Control. Centralized load control systems, whether simple controllers or computers, are capable of reducing demand and energy consumption. Load shedding during the maximum monthly

Table 6-1
KW Multipliers for Power Factor Correction

Original Power Factor	Corrected Power Factor										
	0.90	0.91	0.92	0.93	0.94	0.95	0.96	0.97	0.98	0.99	1.0
0.50	1.248	1.276	1.306	1.337	1.369	1.403	1.440	1.481	1.529	1.589	1.732
0.51	1.203	1.231	1.261	1.292	1.324	1.358	1.395	1.436	1.484	1.544	1.687
0.52	1.159	1.187	1.217	1.248	1.280	1.314	1.351	1.392	1.440	1.500	1.643
0.53	1.116	1.144	1.174	1.205	1.237	1.271	1.308	1.349	1.397	1.457	1.600
0.54	1.075	1.103	1.133	1.164	1.196	1.230	1.267	1.308	1.356	1.416	1.559
0.55	1.035	1.063	1.093	1.124	1.156	1.190	1.227	1.268	1.316	1.376	1.519
0.56	0.996	1.024	1.054	1.085	1.117	1.151	1.188	1.229	1.277	1.337	1.480
0.57	0.958	0.986	1.016	1.047	1.079	1.113	1.150	1.191	1.239	1.299	1.442
0.58	0.921	0.949	0.979	1.010	1.042	1.076	1.113	1.154	1.202	1.262	1.405
0.59	0.885	0.913	0.943	0.974	1.006	1.040	1.077	1.118	1.166	1.226	1.369
0.60	0.849	0.877	0.907	0.938	0.970	1.004	1.041	1.082	1.130	1.190	1.333
0.61	0.815	0.843	0.873	0.904	0.936	0.970	1.007	1.048	1.096	1.156	1.299
0.62	0.782	0.810	0.840	0.871	0.903	0.937	0.974	1.015	1.063	1.123	1.266
0.63	0.749	0.777	0.807	0.838	0.870	0.904	0.941	0.982	1.030	1.090	1.233
0.64	0.717	0.745	0.775	0.806	0.838	0.872	0.909	0.950	0.998	1.068	1.201
0.65	0.685	0.713	0.743	0.774	0.806	0.840	0.877	0.918	0.966	1.026	1.169
0.66	0.654	0.682	0.712	0.743	0.775	0.809	0.846	0.887	0.935	0.995	1.138
0.67	0.624	0.652	0.682	0.713	0.745	0.779	0.816	0.857	0.905	0.965	1.108
0.68	0.594	0.622	0.652	0.683	0.715	0.749	0.786	0.827	0.875	0.935	1.078
0.69	0.565	0.593	0.623	0.654	0.686	0.720	0.757	0.798	0.846	0.906	1.049
0.70	0.536	0.594	0.564	0.625	0.657	0.691	0.728	0.769	0.817	0.877	1.020
0.71	0.508	0.536	0.566	0.597	0.629	0.663	0.700	0.741	0.789	0.849	0.992
0.72	0.480	0.508	0.538	0.569	0.601	0.635	0.672	0.713	0.761	0.821	0.964
0.73	0.452	0.480	0.510	0.541	0.573	0.607	0.644	0.685	0.733	0.793	0.936
0.74	0.425	0.453	0.483	0.514	0.546	0.580	0.617	0.658	0.706	0.766	0.909
0.75	0.398	0.426	0.456	0.487	0.519	0.553	0.590	0.631	0.679	0.739	0.882
0.76	0.371	0.399	0.429	0.460	0.492	0.526	0.563	0.604	0.652	0.712	0.855
0.77	0.345	0.373	0.403	0.434	0.466	0.500	0.537	0.578	0.626	0.686	0.829
0.78	0.318	0.346	0.376	0.407	0.439	0.473	0.510	0.551	0.599	0.659	0.802
0.79	0.292	0.320	0.350	0.381	0.413	0.447	0.484	0.525	0.573	0.633	0.776
0.80	0.266	0.294	0.324	0.355	0.387	0.421	0.458	0.499	0.547	0.609	0.750
0.81	0.240	0.268	0.298	0.329	0.361	0.395	0.432	0.473	0.521	0.581	0.724
0.82	0.214	0.242	0.272	0.303	0.335	0.369	0.406	0.447	0.495	0.555	0.698
0.83	0.188	0.216	0.246	0.277	0.309	0.343	0.380	0.421	0.469	0.529	0.672
0.84	0.162	0.190	0.220	0.251	0.283	0.317	0.354	0.395	0.443	0.503	0.646
0.85	0.136	0.164	0.194	0.225	0.257	0.291	0.328	0.369	0.417	0.477	0.620
0.86	0.109	0.137	0.167	0.198	0.230	0.264	0.301	0.342	0.390	0.450	0.593
0.87	0.083	0.111	0.141	0.172	0.204	0.238	0.275	0.316	0.364	0.424	0.567
0.88	0.056	0.084	0.114	0.145	0.177	0.211	0.248	0.289	0.337	0.397	0.540
0.89	0.028	0.056	0.086	0.117	0.149	0.183	0.220	0.261	0.309	0.369	0.512
0.90	0.000	0.028	0.058	0.089	0.121	0.155	0.192	0.233	0.281	0.341	0.484

Source: Spraque Electric Company, "A Guide to Power Factor Correction for the Plant Engineer," Manual PF-1000, North Adams, MA, 1962, p. 14. Reprinted with permission.

load period, as metered by the power company, reduces the demand charges. The monthly demand savings as a result of load shedding is given by

$$S_d = L_s \times C_d \qquad (6.5)$$

where S_d is the monthly demand savings, L_s is the amount of KW shed to limit power, and C_d is the monthly demand charge in dollars.

Monthly savings can also be computed for reduced energy consumption. As discussed previously, only nonrecoverable loads can be shed/restored with energy savings. The monthly energy savings due to the shed/restore operations of a load is given by

$$S_e = L_s \times t_{off} \times C_e \qquad (6.6)$$

where S_e is the monthly savings, L_s is the KW of the load shed, t_{off} is the off time in hours of the load during the month, and C_e is the monthly energy charge in dollars. The total savings may be computed by summing the savings of all of the nonrecoverable loads.

A secondary savings benefit due to centralized control is that of extended equipment life. Equipment whose life is rated in hours of operation may last longer than normal, thus reducing the number of replacements needed. However, equipment whose life is rated by the number of start/stop operations may wear out quicker. A study of energy savings versus increased maintenance and replacement costs should be made before subjecting these types of loads to centralized control.

Heat Recovery Equipment. Various devices are available for recovering heat that would otherwise be wasted. The recovered heat is then used in other processes within the system. For example, integrated lighting systems utilize waste heat from light sources in conjunction with the comfort conditioning system. In winter, heat that would otherwise be wasted is recovered and circulated into the heating system ducts. In summer, the recovery process reduces the waste heat introduced into the conditioning space, thus lessening the cooling load on the air conditioning system.

Heat recovery is accomplished by (a) refrigeration-type devices and (b) exhaust air equipment.[5] The heat pump is an example of the refrigeration-type process of recovery. The exhaust air recovery process is implemented by four basic devices, including

1. Heat wheels,
2. Heat pipes,
3. Runaround systems, and
4. Air-to-air heat exchangers.

Each of these devices are used to transfer heat from exhaust system air ducts to intake supply air ducts (or vice versa).

Heat wheels and heat pipes require that the two ducts be adjacent. Heat wheels are situated such that half of the disc is positioned in each duct. The heat absorbing, motor-driven wheel is rotated to transfer heat from one duct to the other. Heat pipes, on the other hand, are sealed tubes with each half located in the adjacent air ducts. A refrigerant contained within the tubes transfers heat from one air stream to the other by means of evaporation, migration, and condensation. A "wick" is used to provide a means for condensate return.

The runaround system consists of an air-to-liquid heat exchanger in each duct. A liquid is pumped between the two exchangers through a looped pipe system. Thus, heat is transferred between the heat exchangers by the circulating liquid. Air-to-air heat exchangers are junction cabinets through which the two ducts cross. Small, adjacent passages within the cabinet allow heat to transfer from the warmer duct to the cooler duct by means of conduction.

Once recouped from exhaust gases and transferred to the utilization site, recovered heat is generally of low grade. However, the use of this otherwise wasted energy in support of heat generation could reduce fuel consumption by 20 to 25 percent in various processes.[6]

Selection of Final Plan

Once a system is surveyed, energy wasters identified, and potential energy savings through conservation investigated, a final energy management plan should be constructed. Selected programs should be categorized by expense, order of implementation, and priority for proper initiation as investment capital is available. Alternatives should be considered so as to ensure that the venture will be both a sound investment and a significant energy saving measure.

Financial Considerations

Since business must operate on a budget schedule, large capital expenditures may necessarily be spread out over several years. Capital recovery might be increased by passing on a part of the cost burden to the consumer. For example, a power company might include load management program expenses in the rate base (as is often done for environmental protection costs). The government could share the cost burden by issuing subsidies, grants, and tax relief for progressive energy conservation action in the private and business sectors.

Electrical energy management programs often offer high rates of return and fast payback periods. The following procedures[7] may be used as a first-order economic evaluation to indicate which programs appear profitable. (Attractive programs should then be subjected to a more detailed financial analysis that considers such factors as the time value of money, salvage, and taxes.)

First, the annual monetary savings should be calculated (such as in some of the above programs). The general form for annual savings is given by

$$S = (K \times C) - D \qquad (6.7)$$

where S is the annual dollar savings, K is the annual kilowatt-hour (or demand) savings, C is the forecasted average kilowatt-hour (or demand) charge, and D is any additional operating disbursement (for example, maintenance costs). The payout period is then determined by

$$P = I/S \qquad (6.8)$$

where P is the payout period in years, I is the installed cost of the conservation program, and S is the annual savings from equation (6.7). Typical payout periods required by industries are one to three years.

Next, a straight-line depreciation schedule is calculated by

$$D_{SL} = I/n \qquad (6.9)$$

where D_{SL} is the depreciation expense and n is the predicted life in years. The rate of return (ROR) of the investment is then determined by

$$\%ROR = [(S - D_{SL})/I]\ 100\%. \tag{6.10}$$

The ROR must be greater than or equal to the company's established minimum ROR for acceptance of an investment.

Finally, the present worth or present value of the anticipated series of future savings realized during the life of the project is determined by discounting. Present worth is given by

$$PW = S(PWF) \tag{6.11}$$

where PW is present worth and PWF is the uniform series present worth factor given by

$$PWF = \frac{(1 + i)^n - 1}{i(1 + i)^n} \tag{6.12}$$

where i is the discount interest rate of the business (that is, the minimum acceptable ROR).

Although these calculations may serve as an indication of beneficial energy conservation programs, a detailed financial analysis should be performed to ensure accurate results. The final electrical energy management programs can then be selected.

Top Management Approval

The final plan should be submitted to top management for review and approval. Upon acceptance, the minimal cost energy management programs should be immediately implemented and the large investment programs scheduled in the budget. Reports of potential money and energy savings to management serve as incentive for continued support of the energy management program.

Summary

Energy waste may be attributed to faulty building systems, inefficient equipment, and poor energy-use life styles. Energy audit data
aids in determining such waste. Analysis of various electrical energy
management programs should indicate potential areas for savings.
Such programs may vary over a wide range of expenses.

The more attractive energy management programs should be
subjected to financial analysis to determine if they are economically
feasible. A final selection of programs should be made according to
the business' financial policies. Top management approval should be
acquired for the final plan before program implementation is initiated.

Implementation of energy management programs is discussed in
the next chapter.

7 Electrical Energy Management Program Implementation

Implementation of an electrical energy management program is the actual application of the designed and approved plan. As with any other business action of this nature, the energy programs must be scheduled for initiation, and control must be exerted to maintain the implementation as planned.

Implementation Timetable

Energy management programs fall into three classes of expenditure, often designated by the terms

1. No cost,
2. Low cost, and
3. Extra cost.

No-cost and low-cost programs can typically be implemented in a matter of days or weeks; whereas extra-cost programs often involve (a) long periods of study and evaluation and (b) time frames for ordering, installing, and testing of new facilities. Because of budgetary constraints, extra-cost projects might take months or even years to implement.

Graphical timetables are effective aids for proper sequencing and controlling of energy management programs. Business organizational techniques such as the Gantt chart are commonly used methods for clearly illustrating the events that will occur throughout an implementation schedule. Flow charts and Delta Charts may be helpful in defining program aspects in detail. Care should be taken to allow for delays in the implementation scheme as problems sometimes arise.

Program Evaluation

At the onset of implementation, program performance data should be gathered. Immediate evaluation should be initiated so that the effects of energy conservation efforts can be determined. Any necessary troubleshooting and adjustments can then be made early in the program.

Caution must be exercised when implementing the program as errors could result in little or no savings or possibly even in increased consumption. The following example[1] demonstrates the failure to inspect a system completely before applying energy conservation action. Lighting load in a particular office building was reduced by disconnecting one-half of the light fixtures. Little or no energy savings was realized. However, a full examination of the electrical and air conditioning systems revealed that the air conditioning electric reheat coils were designed to operate automatically (by means of thermostat controls) and that these coils were activated when the lighting fixtures were isolated from the system. This example stresses the need for a comprehensive survey of all systems and their integrated connections before an energy management program is even designed.

Actual energy savings should be compared to the theoretical savings and the deviation between the two minimized (unless, of course, more energy is saved than anticipated). The energy savings objectives set early in the program may take a few months to achieve. As savings goals are reached, new targets should be set until the conservation savings are optimized.

Program Maintenance

The electrical energy management program will be effective only if the established objectives and procedures are maintained. Continued evaluation of the program's contents and effectiveness should be made at regular intervals (that is, monthly, quarterly, and annually). Energy action correspondence with top management should be kept current.

A large-scale energy management program may justify a need for the development of an energy budget; therefore, future program expansions and operating expenses should be carefully planned. Energy budget costs might also include hiring of additional energy management personnel.

Education plays an important role in the energy picture. The energy management group should stay abreast of the state-of-the-art by reading literature, participating in seminars and workshops, and trading case histories and ideas among members. Personnel should be trained in energy management theory and application so that the expertise needed to maintain the energy programs will always be available.

Summary

The final plan of energy management programs is put into action according to an implementation schedule or timetable. Minimal cost programs can be implemented upon approval; whereas large invest-ment programs may take years to put into effect completely. Evaluation of program performance should begin immediately with implementation so that proper control can be exerted. Energy savings goals take time to achieve; therefore, early troubleshooting of problem areas will cause savings to occur sooner. The energy programs should be maintained by continually monitoring program performance, by training energy management personnel, and by investigating new conservation measures as they arise.

8   Overview

This work has attempted to view the breadth of electrical energy management as it applies to commercial and industrial business establishments. The following summary will highlight the more prominent *aspects* of this work.

The energy sources currently utilized in the United States are limited. New sources will be required in the future to meet our nation's energy demand. Conservation of energy serves as a means of buying time by helping to preserve depletable raw fuels. Conservation of electrical energy is indeed an effective means of reducing the rate of energy consumption.

The largest energy savings can be affected by the business community. However, for a business to implement a large-scale conservation program, two possible problem areas might have to be resolved. The first is that of top management commitment. Management must be convinced that energy conservation is essential. With rising energy costs, the potential savings of conservation measures thus serves as a primary incentive for management support. Public relations with consumers are often fortified as a result of business endeavors in energy management. The second potential problem is that of available capital for energy management programs. Large-scale programs sometimes involve significant investments that might be constrained by the company's budget. However, many energy conservation projects may actually be considered profitable investments because of the drastic savings that can be realized.

Before practical energy management programs can be selected, an audit of the electrical network's energy consumption performance must be conducted. The audit should indicate potential areas for savings. The audit might also indicate that certain portions of the system are operating near maximum possible efficiencies; therefore, investments in conservation measures might not be economically feasible. The energy audit thus serves as a basis for singling out programs and comparing energy consumption patterns before and after conservation action is implemented.

Electrical energy conservation is achieved by reducing overall energy consumption and by adjusting energy consumption patterns through load management. Load management programs attempt to maintain the overall demand for electrical energy at a constant level. Many load management projects require a cooperative effort between the utility and the customer to be beneficial for both parties.

The types of electrical energy management programs to be administered by a business depend primarily on the conservation opportunities available within the particular plant or buildings. The most advantageous programs should be selected and implemented as quickly as possible. The savings from successful programs serve as a perpetual incentive for top management support of energy conservation management programs. Program maintenance is essential for the continuation of optimal energy management program performance.

The need for electrical management (as well as total energy management) has developed primarily because of the energy crisis. The days of cheap energy are gone forever. From now on, energy management will be the key to optimizing both the present energy supplies and the future energy resources.

Notes

Notes

Chapter 1
Introduction

1. "Top Scientists Call for Nuclear and Coal," *Watts Cookin',* Public Service Indiana, April 1975, p. 7.

2. Energy Research and Development Administration, "Creating Energy Choices for the Future," Washington, D.C., 1975, p. 29.

3. D.C. Burnham, "A Shift to an Electric Economy Must Be the Heart of America's Energy Policy," A Westinghouse Advertisement, 1973.

4. U.S. Department of Commerce, "How to Start an Energy Management Program," Washington, D.C., Government Printing Office, October 1973.

5. Ross Whitehead, "Design to Save Energy," *Industry Week,* July 9, 1973, p. 22.

Chapter 2
Energy Management Consideration

1. U.S. Department of Commerce, "Industry's Vital Stake in Energy Management," Washington, D.C., Government Printing Office, May 1974.

2. Norman Peach, "Do You Understand Demand Charges?" *Power,* September 1970.

3. Guy W. Gupton, Jr., "Heat Conservation Systems: Workable? Economical?" *Energy Management,* Indiana Electric Association, Section I-A, p. 5.

4. Carl H. Bauman, "Organizing for Energy Management at the Corporate and Plant Levels," *The 1975 Energy Management Guidebook* (New York: McGraw-Hill, 1975), p. 29.

5. Ibid., p. 30.

6. "The Delta Chart: A Method for R & D Project Portrayal," *IEEE Transactions on Engineering Management,* November 1971, p. 42.

Chapter 3
Electrical Load Analysis

1. Federal Energy Administration, "Lighting and Thermal Operations Guidelines," FEA-195-D, Washington, D.C., Government Printing Office, 1975, p. 1.

2. Harold Pender and William A. Del Mar, *Electrical Engineer's Handbook Electric Power*, 4th ed. (New York: John Wiley and Sons, Inc., 1949), Section 15, p. 29.

3. General Electric Company, "High Intensity Discharge Lamps," TP-109, Cleveland, August 1971, pp. 4, 10.

4. U.S. Department of Commerce, "Energy Labeling of Household Appliances," NBS LC 1054, A Joint Advertisement with the National Bureau of Standards, Washington, D.C., 1975.

5. Edison Electric Institute, *Electric Application Handbook, for Commercial Salesmen*, New York, 1972, Section I, p. 3.

6. R.L. Dunning, "Furnace-Efficiency Variations Explained," *Electric World*, February 1974, p. 61.

7. *Energy Alternatives: A Comparative Analysis*, Catalog Number PREX 14.2:EN2, Washington, D.C., Government Printing Office, May 1975, Section 13, p. 16.

8. Honeywell, Inc., *Energy Conservation Management Workshop*, Minneapolis, 1975, Section IV-B, p. 2.

9. Cam Industries, Inc., "Electrode Boilers," Bulletin 400, 1974, p. 2.

10. Edison Electric Institute, *Electric Application Handbook, for Commercial Salesmen*, Section III, p. 2.

11. Pender, *Electrical Engineer's Handbook Electric Power*, Section 18, p. 42.

12. Edison Electric Institute, *Power Sales Manual*, New York, 1959, Chapter 38, p. 6.

13. Ibid., Chapter 35, 1952, p. 2.

14. Honeywell, Inc., *Energy Conservation Management Workshop*, Section IV-B, p. 2.

15. G.L. Oscarson, *ABC of Large Motors and Control*, Electric Machinery Manufacturing Co., 1973, Part 2, Applications, p. 5.

16. Westinghouse Electric Corporation, *Distribution Systems*, 2nd ed., East Pittsburg, 1965, p. 24.

17. Ibid., p. 25.

Chapter 4
Electrical Energy Auditing

1. Robert R. Gatts, Robert G. Massey, and John C. Robertson, *Energy Conservation Guide for Industry and Commerce (EPIC)*, Catalog Number C13.11:115, Washington, D.C., Government Printing Office, September 1974, Section 2, p. 18.

2. " 'Who's Wasting Energy?'," *Electrified Industry* 39 (November 1975): 8-9.

Chapter 5
Load Management Techniques

1. Kurt Cogliatti, *A Load Management System*, New York, Landis and Gyr Corp., 1974, p. 2.

2. Digital Equipment Corp., "Power Management," EA 04744 750100/46, Maynard, MA, 1975.

3. "Saves Energy, Saves Dollars," *Electrified Industry* 38 (October 1974): 23.

4. Digital Equipment Corp., "Power Demand Control System User's Guide," DEC-11-APDUA-A-D, Maynard, MA, Section 1, p. 2.

5. Ibid., p. 3.

6. Richard H. McConeghy, "Demand Control, Control to Reduce Monthly Electric Bills," Milwaukee, WI, Square D Co., November 1973, p. 4.

7. "Power Demand Control," *Electrified Industry* 38 (October 1974): 19.

8. John Peschon and Leif Isaksen, *Electric Power Systems Analysis Research*, Palo Alto, CA, Systems Control, Inc., July 1974, p. 152.

9. "Company's Load Research Committee Studies Customer Energy Use," *Watts Cookin'*, Public Service Indiana, March 1976, p. 8.

10. "Radio Controls Home Energy Loads," *Transmission and Distribution* 27 (October 1975): 13.

11. "European Ripple Load Control Comes to Vermont," *Transmission and Distribution* 28 (January 1976): 22.

12. Bruce L. Jaffee, "Future Changes in Electric Utility Rate Structures," *Public Utilities Fortnightly* 95 (April 10, 1975): 27-30.

13. W.W. Pleines, "Transformer Load Management," *Transmission and Distribution* 16 (March 1964): 26.

14. C.W. Crane, "Feeder Load Management System," *Transmission and Distribution* 26 (October 1974): 34, 36.

Chapter 6
Electrical Energy Management Program Design

1. Robert R. Gatts, Robert G. Massey, and John C. Robertson, *Energy Conservation Guide for Industry and Commerce (EPIC)*, Catalog Number C13.11:115, Washington, D.C., Government Printing Office, September 1974, Section 3, p. 18.

2. Edison Electric Institute, *Power Sales Manual*, New York, 1963, Chapter 5, pp. 125, 126.

3. General Electric Company, "Lighting Maintenance," TP-105, Cleveland, January 1969, p. 8.

4. Ibid., pp. 5, 6.

5. "The Energy Misers Part Two," *Modern Schools*, November 1973, pp. 8, 9.

6. *Energy Alternatives: A Comparative Analysis*, Catalog Number PREX 14.2:EN2, Washington, D.C., Government Printing Office, May 1975, Section 13, p. 32.

7. Gatts, *Energy Conservation Guide for Industry and Commerce*, Section 5, pp. 1-4.

Chapter 7
Electrical Energy Management Program Implementation

1. Syska and Hennessy, Inc., "Don't Switch Off That Light . . . ," *Syska and Hennessy Technical Letter* 24, no. 1, January 1974, New York.

Bibliography

Bauman, Carl H., "Organizing For Energy Management at the Corporate and Plant Levels," in *The 1975 Energy Management Guidebook*, New York, McGraw-Hill, 1975, pp. 29-31.

Burnham, D.C., "A Shift to an Electric Economy Must Be the Heart of America's Energy Policy," A Westinghouse Corporation Advertisement, 1973.

Cam Industries, Inc., "Electrode Boilers," Bulletin 400, 1974.

Chevron Oil Company, *Energy Conservation Facts.*

Cogliatti, Kurt, *A Load Management System,* New York, Landis and Gyr Corporation, 1974.

"Company's Load Research Committee Studies Customer Energy Use," *Watts Cookin'*, Public Service Indiana, March 1976, p. 8.

Crane, C.W., "Feeder Load Management System," *Transmission and Distribution* 26 (October 1974): 34-36.

Digital Equipment Corporation, "Power Demand Control System User's Guide," DEC-11-APDUA-A-D, Maynard, MA.

Digital Equipment Corporation, "Power Management," EA 04744 750100/46, Maynard, MA, 1975.

Dunning, R.L., "Furnace-Efficiency Variations Explained," *Electrical World*, February 1, 1974, pp. 60-62.

Edison Electric Institute, "Annual Energy Requirements of Electric Household Appliances," EEI-Pub #75-61, New York, 1975.

Edison Electric Institute, *Electric Application Handbook for Commercial Salesmen*, New York, 1972.

Edison Electric Institute, *Power Sales Manual*, New York.

Energy Alternatives: A Comparative Analysis Catalog Number PREX 14.2:EN2, Washington, D.C., Government Printing Office, May 1975.

Energy Research and Development Administration, "Creating Energy Choices for the Future," Washington, D.C., 1975.

"European Ripple Load Control Comes to Vermont," *Transmission and Distribution* 28 (January 1976): 22.

Federal Energy Administration, "Lighting and Thermal Operations Guidelines," FEA-195-D, Washington, D.C., Government Printing Office, 1975.

Gatts, Robert R., Massey, Robert G., and Robertson, John C., *Energy Conservation Guide for Industry and Commerce (EPIC)*,

Catalog Number C13.11:115, Washington, D.C., Government Printing Office, September 1974.

General Electric Company, "High Intensity Discharge Lamps," TP-109, Cleveland, August 1971.

General Electric Company, "Lighting Maintenance," TP-105, Cleveland, January 1969.

"Getting Power From Here to There Efficiently," *Electrified Industry* 39 (July 1975): 7-9.

Gupton, Guy W., Jr., "Heat Conservation Systems: Workable? Economical?" *Energy Management*, Indiana Electric Association, Section 1-A.

Honeywell, Inc., *Energy Conservation Management Workshop*, Minneapolis, 1975.

ITE Imperial Corporation, " 'Watt-Watcher' Application Manual," Bulletin No. 6.12.2-2A, Wilmington, MA.

Jaffee, Bruce L., "Future Changes in Electric Utility Rate Structures," *Public Utilities Fortnightly* 95 (April 10, 1975): 25-30.

Kaufman, J.E. (ed), *IES Lighting Handbook*, Illuminating Engineering Society, 5th ed., 1972.

McConeghy, Richard H., "Demand Control, Control to Reduce Monthly Electric Bills," Milwaukee, WI, Square D Company, November 1973.

McGraw-Edison, "The ABC of Capacitors."

National Electrical Manufacturers Association and National Electrical Contractors Association, *Total Energy Management.*

Oscarson, G.L., *ABC of Large AC Motors and Control*, Minneapolis, MN, Electric Machinery Manufacturing Co., 1973.

Peach, Norman, "Do You Understand Demand Charges?" *Power*, September 1970.

Pender, Harold and Del Mar, William A., *Electrical Engineers' Handbook Electric Power*, 4th ed., New York, John Wiley and Sons, Inc., 1949.

Peschon, John and Isaksen, Leif, *Electric Power Systems Analysis Research*, Palo Alto, CA, July 1974.

Pleines, W.W., "Transformer Load Management," *Transmission and Distribution* 16 (March 1964): 26-28, 32-33.

"Power Demand Control," *Electrified Industry* 38 (October 1974): 19-22.

"Radio Controls Home Energy Loads," *Transmission and Distribution* 27 (October 1975): 13.

Sangamo Electric Company, "Power Capacitors: What They Can Do," Springfield, IL.

"Saves Energy, Saves Dollars," *Electrified Industry* 38 (October 1974): 23.

Sprague Electric Company, "A Guide to Power Factor Correction for the Plant Engineer," Manual PF-1000, North Adams, MA, 1962.

Syska and Hennessy, Inc., "Don't Switch Off That Light . . . ," *Syska and Hennessy Technical Letter* 24, no. 1, January 1974, New York.

"The Delta Chart: A Method of R & D Project Portrayal," *IEEE Transactions on Engineering Management*, November 1971, pp. 42-50.

"The Energy Misers Part Two," *Modern Schools*, November 1973, pp. 8-9.

"Top Scientists Call for Nuclear and Coal," *Watts Cookin'*, Public Service Indiana, April 1975, p. 7.

U.S. Department of Commerce, "Energy Labeling of Household Appliances," A Joint Advertisement with the National Bureau of Standards, NBS LC1054, Washington, D.C., 1975.

U.S. Department of Commerce, "How to Start an Energy Management Program," Washington, D.C., Government Printing Office, October 1973.

U.S. Department of Commerce, "Industry's Vital Stake in Energy Management," Washington, D.C., Government Printing Office, May 1974.

U.S. Department of Commerce, *Technical Options for Energy Conservation in Buildings,* Catalog Number C13.46:789, Washington, D.C., Government Printing Office, July 1973.

Westinghouse Electric Corporation, *Distribution Systems,* 2nd ed., East Pittsburg, 1965.

Whitehead, Ross, "Design to Save Energy," *Industry Week*, July 9, 1973, pp. 22-26.

" 'Who's Wasting Energy?'," *Electrified Industry* 39 (November 1975): 8-11.

Index

Index

About the Authors

Lawrence J. Vogt is a senior industrial marketing engineer for Public Service Indiana. He received the B.S. and the M.Eng. with specialization in the field of electrical engineering from the University of Louisville. His work experience includes distribution design and industrial power engineering. He is a member of the Institute of Electrical and Electronic Engineers and the Society of Manufacturing Engineers and an associate member of the American Society of Heating, Refrigerating, and Air Conditioning Engineers.

David A. Conner is assistant dean for research of the Speed Scientific School of the University of Louisville and associate professor of electrical engineering and computer science. He received the B.S. and M.S. degrees from Auburn University and the Ph.D. from the Georgia Institute of Technology. Dr. Conner has served on the faculties of Auburn University, Georgia Institute of Technology, and the University of Tennessee at Chattanooga, and has been employed by the International Business Machines Corporation. He is a registered professional engineer in Georgia, Tennessee, and Kentucky and has served as a consultant to over twenty corporations. He is a senior member of the Institute of Electrical and Electronic Engineers and a member of the American Society for Engineering Education, the American Association of University Professors, and the Kentucky Society of Professional Engineers.